Millersville, Wisconsin

Sheboygan County Historical Research Center
with Millersville Area Committee

Arline Hoppe, Rita Milbrath, Robert Spindler
and Violet Usadel

Millersville
Wisconsin

A compilation of news articles,
memories and photos
of the area before
incorporation with Howards Grove

Sheboygan County Historical Research Center with
Millersville Area Research Committee
Arline Hoppe, Rita Milbrath, Robert Spindler and Violet Usadel

Millersville Avenue- Early 1900s - looking east

Millersville, Wisconsin, now a part of the village of Howards Grove in Sheboygan County, was for decades its own settlement. The history of the community dates back to 1846 when the first immigrants found their way along the Pigeon River and settled in the area.

At first the two settlements were known as Howards and Mueller Villa, later becoming Howards Grove and Millersville. On August 1, 1967, the two communities incorporated as Howards Grove - Millersville, becoming Sheboygan County's 10th village, the fourth largest. It also brought the village fame with its cumbersome 24-letter title, the longest in the state.

The name controversy created quite a stir beginning in the spring of 1967 when residents rejected such fanciful proposals as "Forward" and "Harmony". The issue apparently has been settled. A vote in 1972 officially married the Millersvillians to Howards Grove. Howards Grove became the official name.

This book is a compilation of news articles, stories, remembrances and histories of the people, business and activities of the area.

Millersville Avenue- 1914- looking west

'Marries' Howards Grove
November 2, 1971
Plymouth Review
Mrs. Elsie Karstaedt
Correspondent

Howards Grove- Howards Grove-Millersville has lost the distinction of being the "long name capital" of Wisconsin. Electors went to the polls Tuesday and the majority decided to name the 998 population community Howards Grove – one of three choices on the ballot.

The results: Howards Grove- 313; Riverside- 190; and Howards Grove-Millersville- 4. None of the 507 residents who voted wrote in any other name.

Harold Kimme, village president, said he was gratified with the large voter turnout. "Eighty-five percent of the eligible voters came to the polls. The majority voted for the name Howards Grove, and I hope everyone will work together in promoting our village and the name Howards Grove," he said.

… History of the community dates back to 1846 when the first immigrants found their way along the Pigeon River and settled in the area. At first the two settlements were known as Howards and Mueller Villa, later becoming Howards Grove and Millersville.

Four years ago, on August 1, 1967, the two communities incorporated as Howards Grove-Millersville, becoming Sheboygan County's 10th village, the fourth largest. It also brought the village fame with its cumbersome 24-letter title, the longest in the state.

… The name controversy has been raging ever since the spring of 1967 when residents rejected such fanciful proposals as "Forward" and "Harmony". The issue apparently has been settled now with Millersvillians officially "married" to Howards Grove.

An aerial view of Millersville in 1950 looking northwest.

Millersville- A Brief History

The Sheboygan Press
December 1, 1953
Norma Kaemmer

'Millersville, Die Kleine Stadt Die blos Eine Sidwalk Hat'

(Millersville, the little town that only has one sidewalk)

This German saying has been heard many times through the past years and nicely describes the little village of Millersville, situated on County Trunk JJ and Highway 32. The intersection is right in the center of the village proper.

Millersville has a population of approximately 260 people, living in 48 homes that are housing 63 separate families. Except for perhaps 15 families, who have moved there in recent years, they are all related. About 20 families are living in the same houses either with parents, brothers or sisters. Most of all of them are direct descendants of the earliest settlers and still live in the old pioneer homes. Thirteen of the oldest residents have all their children and their respective families living either in the same upstairs or downstairs apartments or next door to them. Thirteen separate families are closely related, and in them thirty-one people bear the name Sprenger, so that the village at the present date might well be called Sprengerville.

The history of Millersville, however, dates back to 1846. In order to relate its founding and early history, one must date back to 1846. Most, if not all of the town's early pioneers, came from Germany. The German language is still prevalent, especially in the Millersville area.

Pigeon River Calls

Way back, the first white man to come to Wisconsin was a Frenchman, who crossed the ocean, and by way of the Gulf and Great Lakes came into Green Bay. In that way others followed and immigrated farther down the state until Town Herman was reached. It seems all immigrants came by water and followed lakes, rivers and streams. Thus, it was the Pigeon River that beckoned the early Millersville settlers.

At that time Indians lived in wigwams all along the Pigeon River. The only road at first was an Indian path, which became the Green Bay road and is now Highway 32. Town Herman was then an unbroken wilderness. With the assistance of an ax and fire brand, the first settlers cut trees and built small, crude log cabins. In later years more clearings were made. The nearest neighbor was then three to four miles away.

It was the fall of 1846 that the first settlers came from Germany and formed a Lipper settlement (hailing from Lippe-Detmold). Among the first to arrive were F. Beckfield, D. Nordholz, Fr. Binder, C. Meyer, George Pieper, F. Prigge, Wm. Kalk, H. Mahlstedt and Ernst W. Schlichting. Because Schlichting owned all the land of section 35, he was known as Der Bush Koenig. When Charles Oetling came in fall 1847 he purchased some of that land which is now part of Millersville. At that time also Henry Mueller came, and he purchased land along the Pigeon River where he erected his home and the first saw and grist mill on the entire property where a box company is now situated. In 1854 Mueller purchased the entire village land in Section 26. This was laid out in lots, and sold in time to the incoming settlers. Thus, as business progressed and more homes were built the area became known as Mueller Villa. In later years it became Millersville. More and more settlers arrived in Town Herman and settled in sections 26 and 35 around the Millersville vicinity. Among them were Wm. Heuer, Carl Henning, August Bohlmann, John Dengel and John Kohl.

The entire area of Town Herman was at first named after Herman Howard, one of the first settlers. Then it was changed to Howard, which later became the village Howards Grove, when the Herman vicinity became separate villages in 1848.

The first town meeting was held at the Howard's Hotel with Charles Oetling being named the first chairman. His son, Otto, was the first white child born in town Herman. Otto Oetling was born in the pioneer Oetling home situated on the southwest corner of Millersville.

The first school district was organized in 1848 with the first school classes held in an annex to the Oetling home. Miss Eva Atwood was the first teacher and her salary was $32 a month. She taught a five to six month term.

The present school building, though lately added to and remodeled, was erected across the street from the Oetling home. Carl Bohlmann was the contractor and its construction cost was $355. Charles Oetling was the first director of the school board.

The first post office was founded in 1849 by E.W. Schlichting and was situated a mile north at Howards. From there the villagers and surrounding farmers got mail once or twice a week. Most of it was delivered on foot. It was nothing to travel several miles at the time in the worst of weather conditions.

Another aerial view of Millersville about 1950 looking southwest.

First Business

The first church was organized by Pastor Sprengling. He was succeeded in 1860 by Pastor Kleinhans. St. Paul's Lutheran church was built in 1884 by William Kohl, contractor. It has only this year been remodeled and a new organ installed.

The first store in Millersville was built by William Kohl, contractor. He was the son of pioneer John Kohl, born in 1853. William Kohl also erected a wagon and carpenter shop next to the store in 1870. He built many of the village homes and farm and business buildings.

The first blacksmith shop was owned by Charles Reische. He sold it to Rudolph Schorer in 1902 who operated it for 50 years retiring in 1952.

In 1854 founder Henry G. Mueller erected the first grist and saw mill on the bank of the Pigeon River on the east side of the village. Later a cheese box factory was built in connection with it. When Mueller was elected sheriff of Sheboygan he moved to Sheboygan and sold the box factory and mill to Herman Sprenger.

Mueller's son Henry took over the farm and home and at present his grandson Henry is residing with his family in the old pioneer home. Another grandson, Walter Mueller, has been secretary of the box company since 1926 and resides next door to the pioneer homestead in a newly built home.

Community Hall

The first cheese factory was operated by Adam Kuentz. Cheese was made by various cheese makers until about 1940. In 1942 the building was sold. Its upper flat had formerly been used as a social center known as the old Community Hall.

When William Damrow purchased land in the early 1900s, he erected a tavern on the village corner. It was operated by his son-in-law and daughter Mr. and Mrs. Otto Sprenger. It is now operated by a granddaughter, Mrs. Alfred Doro and her son James. A grandson Frederick Sprenger now owns the farm and resides in the old Damrow home which is an annex to the tavern and hall.

The tinsmith shop situated between the store and tavern on the south side of the village street was built by Arno Usadel. Upon his death, his cousin Roland Neumann took over.

Millersville Brats

Adolph Bohlmann had been the village butcher. His slaughter house stands just back of his home next to the old blacksmith shop. Millersville was noted for its famous bratwurst and summer sausage. Bohlmann had also been the village painter and decorator for many years and almost until the last year had been very active so that every one marveled at his aptitude and endurance.

Henry Berth built the Millersville garage in 1924 and operated it for quite a number of years. At present the building is used as a beer depot.

Adjoining the garage is the village barbershop, owned and operated by Otto Schneider, barber since 1929.

Gust Wiedmeyer and son are the village carpenter and contractors. Their shop is situated next to the barbershop and garage or depot building and is in business since 1916.

The Millersville fire house is situated on the north side of the village main street next to the Schorer home. The fire department was organized in 1923 and has two modern trucks and fire fighting equipment and machinery. Their fire fighting squad is on call day and night. Its first officers were Adolph Bohlmann, president; Rudolph Shorer, chief and vice-president; Alfred Bitter, secretary-treasurer and Wm. Prigge and Gust. Wiedemcycr, directors. The fire department purchased land along the river and made it into a spacious picnic grounds and park now used for many occasions.

Community Project

In 1937 August Knoener drilled an artesian well on his property south of the village, now owned by Nelson Kuhn. It became a community project when the Millersville Recreational Association was organized. They were commonly called, "Pond Diggers" because an 80 x 125 foot bathing pool was made. This was fed by the artesian well.

A driveway was made which leads into and around the firemen's park. Two bath houses were built, a ball diamond made and several sets of floodlights erected. Baseball games provide many an evening's enjoyment for the Millersville and neighboring sport fans.

There are three farms right within the village. One is the pioneer founder's (Henry Mueller) farm operated by his grandson, Henry Mueller the third, the other the pioneer farm now operated by Albert Oetling, son of the first white man born at Millersville and in town Herman. The other is that operated by Frederick Sprenger, also the grandson of one of the earlier residents.

On the village boundary is the pioneer Pieper farm on which a grandson Arthur Pieper resides. His brother, also a grandson of the pioneer is Otto Pieper, who with his son Elmer, operate a farm right across the road. The next farm north about a fourth mile is the old pioneer Kalk farm, operated until last year by Martin Boeldt. To the east of the village is the old Prigge farm, operated also by the pioneer's grandson Hugo Wuestenhagen. To the south and west of the village are other pioneer farms of town Herman being operated by grandsons.

Organizations

The first basketball team was organized in 1920 and its first players were August Dedow, Gerhard Herzog, Philip Horneck, Adolph Kaemmer, Otto Schomberg, Erwin Wehrmann and Erwin Wuestenhagen. There has been a baseball team for many years. It had a Rod and Gun Club and a Women's Homemakers Club for many years.

Its fire fighting squad consists of volunteers and they meet for practice regularly. It has a Recreational Association, a parent teacher association, bowling teams, a girl's 4-H club and many other individual clubs.

Millersville's progress can be credited to the fact that it has since its founding been a manufacturing center, where cheese boxes, lumber and building materials are made.

Other Tidbits by Arline Hoppe

The early pioneers built and lived in homes in the village, but most of the farmland lay west of the village, this following the same method or way it was in the "old country". After the morning milking was done, the cows would be herded to the farm land west of the village. Then later in the afternoon, someone would have to get the cows again for milking. The Otto Sprenger and Mueller cows had to cross Highway 42- now Highway 32, and the Mueller cows would continue through Millersville into the Millersville Box Company driveway and over to the Mueller barn. Many deposits were left along the road and an appropriate name was given to the road to correspond with the mess left on the road.

Most of the early settlers came from Germany and even in the 1920s many child could only speak German when they started school. This created quite a problem for the teachers. Even today the German language is still being used by people in the area.

Two Communities Become One

Millersville and Howards Grove were two small communities in the Town of Herman and in 1962 the Millersville-Howards Grove Sanitary District was formed. Several years later it became obvious for municipal and economic reasons to be combined into one village. These two villages had a history of being very competitive, especially in the field of sports. To become one village didn't sit well with many. And then a new name would have to be chosen, not Howards Grove, not Millersville, but a new short name.

Three couples from each community were selected to study name possibilities. The Howards Grove area had a larger population than the Millersville area, as only a few homes were along Highway 32 and along Millersville Road, the rest of the area was mostly farmland. Of the 329 votes cast, Howards Grove received 175 and Riverside 136. Other names receiving votes were Alpine, Forward and Harmony.

On August 1, 1967 Howards Grove-Millersville became an incorporated village with a population of 927. We then had the distinction of having the longest name in the State of Wisconsin. In 1971 residents voted again to shorten the name- of the 507 votes cast- Howards Grove 313, Riverside 190, Howards Grove-Millersville 4. We retained some of our identity as our main street was named Millersville Avenue.

1862 Sheboygan County Map showing the Millersville area.

1875 Sheboygan County Map showing Millersville area

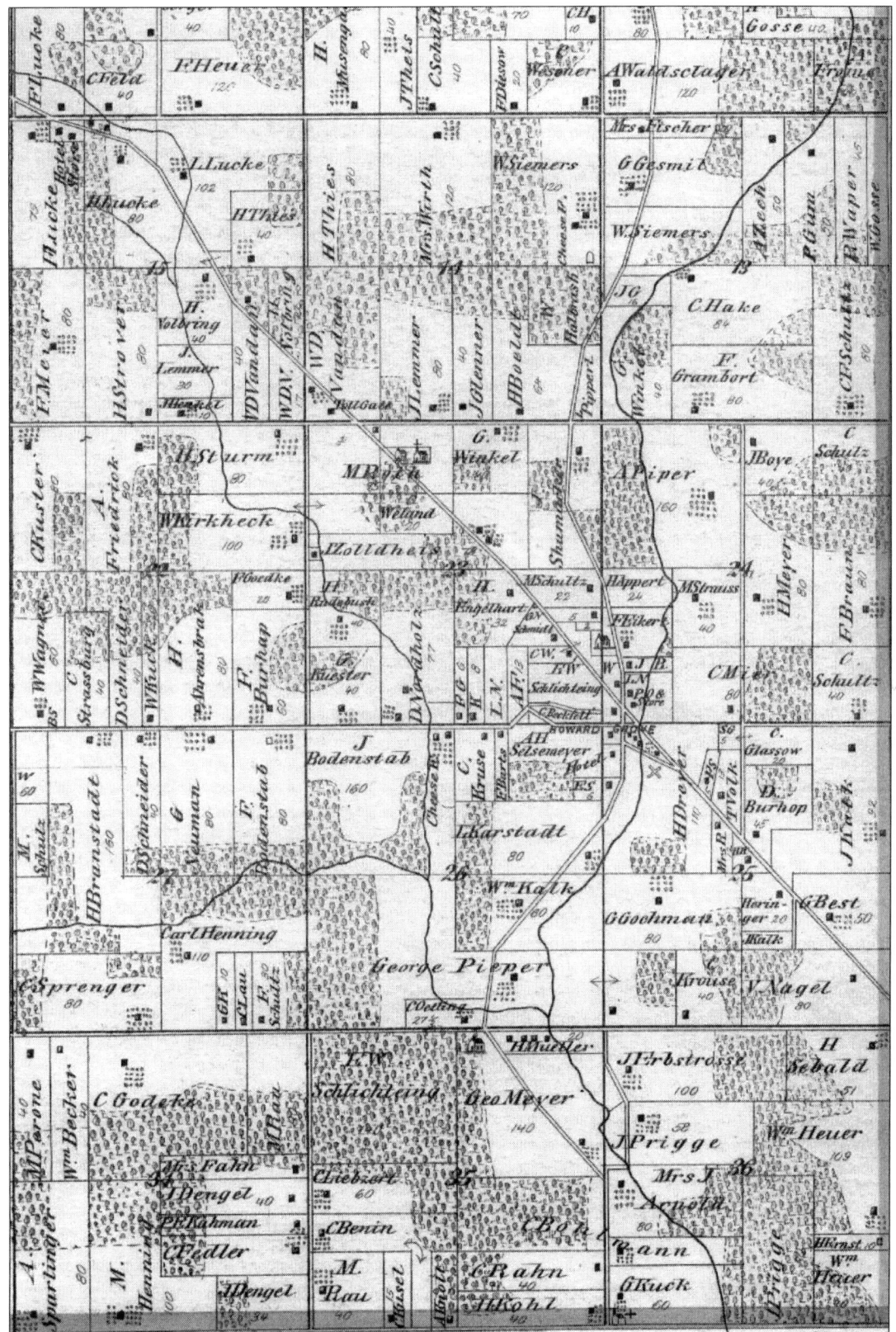

1889 Sheboygan County Plat map showing the Millersville area.

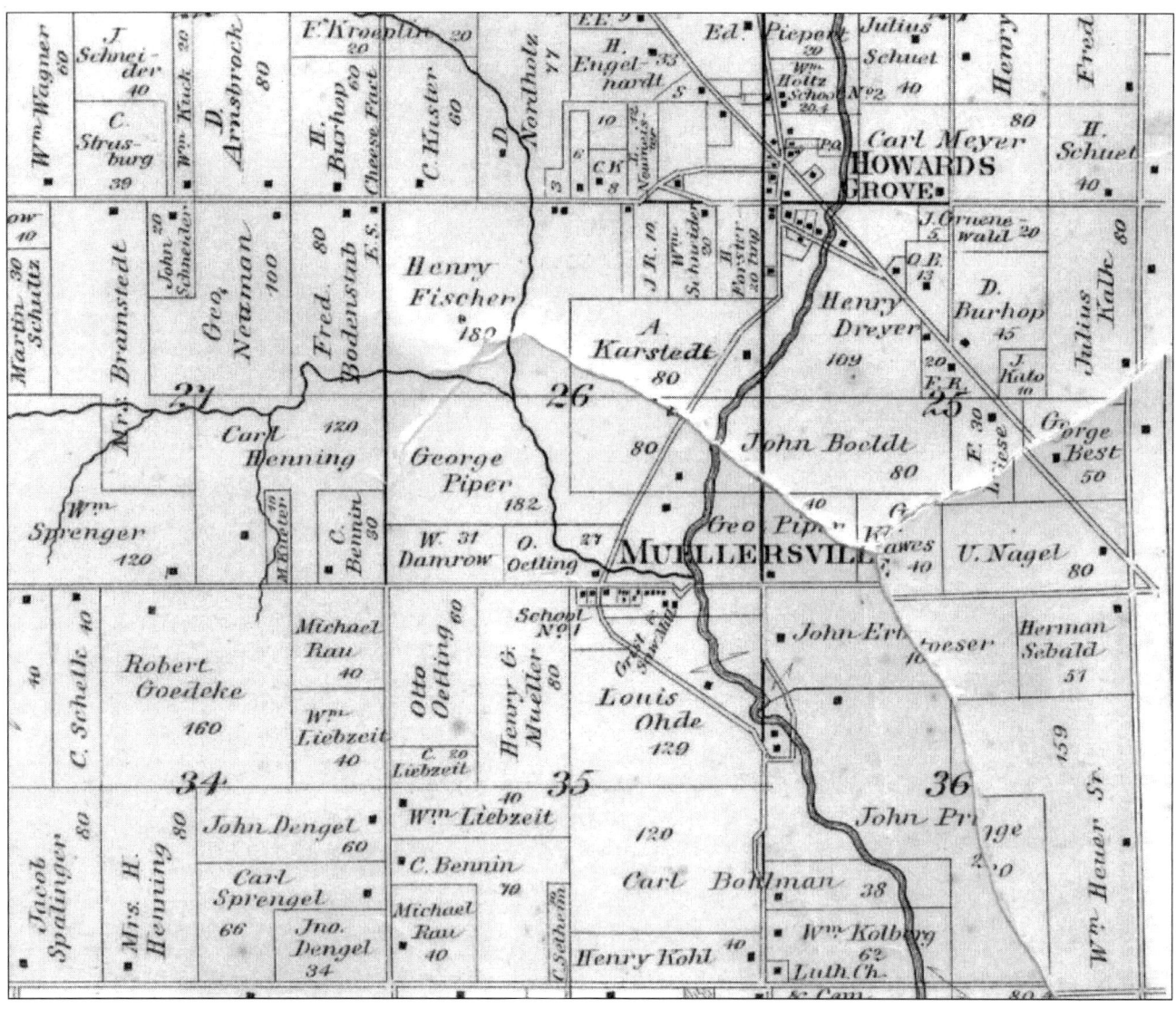

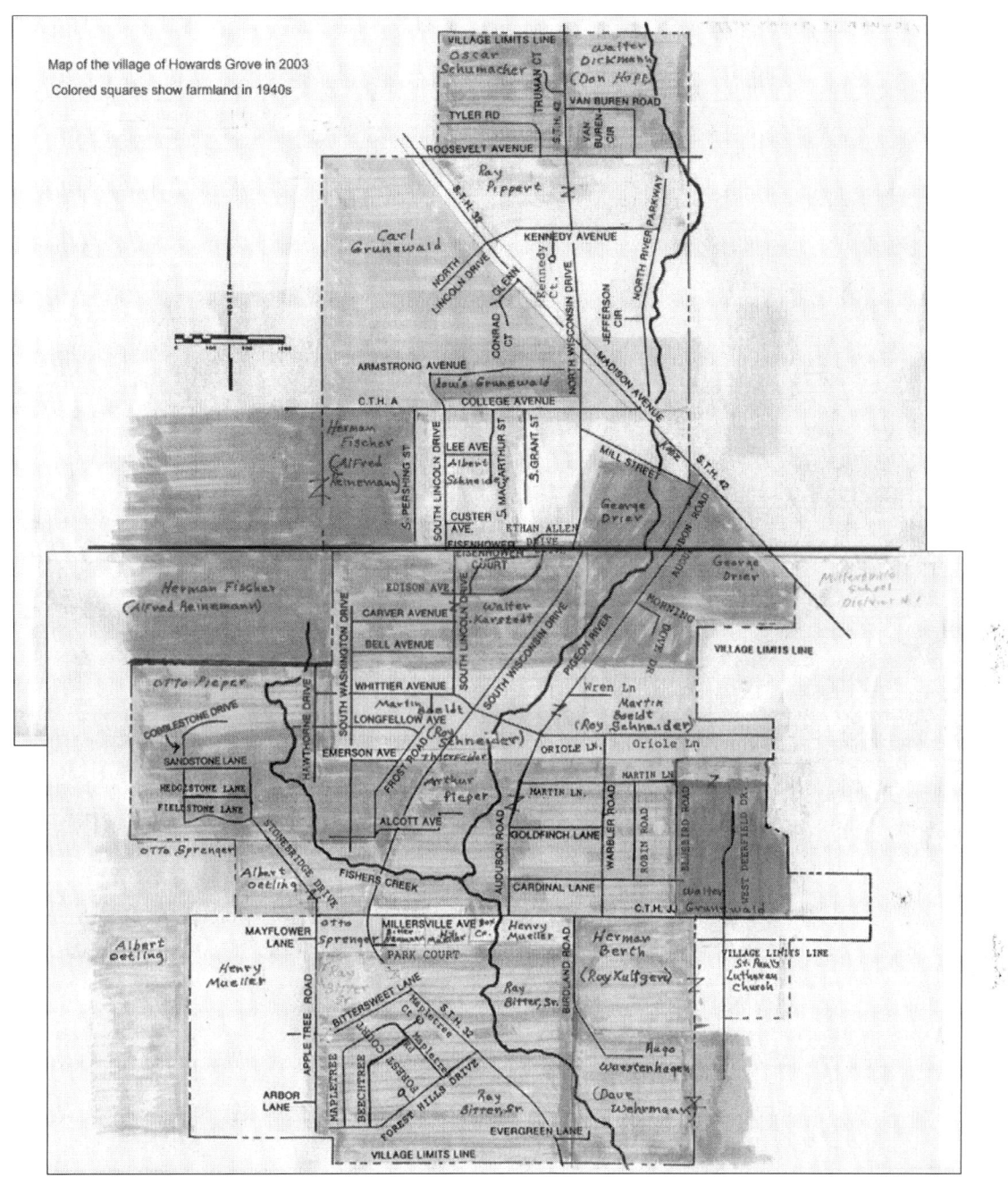

This map of the Millersville area shows the pieces of property owned by early settlers surrounding the intersection of Millersville Avenue and State Highway 32. The area below the horizontal line midway through the picture shows the old Millersville School District.

First Families

This history of Millersville dates back to the fall of 1847 when Charles Oetling came to this area and purchased some of the land in the present Millersville area. At that time also, at the age of 11, Henry G. Mueller came with his parents, the Christian Muellers. Henry Mueller is the namesake of Millersville.

This image shows the Oetling farm located in the heart of Millersville. Great Grandpa Charles Oetling is in the back near the house window. Owner Otto Oetling stands near his team of horses at left. Grandma Anna Oetling is standing next to the window. Great Grandma Johanna Voss Oetling, Great Grandma Helma Dexheimer, Albert Oetling, Adela Gruenwald stand in front next to the gate.

Otto Oetling, son of Charles Oetling and the first child of European immigrants born in the town of Herman.

Henry G. Mueller, born in Germany on May 27, 1836 and came to America with his family in 1847. In 1854 he purchased all the land that would later be included within the boundaries of Millersville. After he laid out lots and sold them the town was called Mueller Villa. It later became Millersville.

He was married in the town of Herman in April of 1861 to Minnie Damrow who was also born in Germany. The couple had ten children including Albert, Louis, Emma, Henry, Adele, Otto, Minnie, Ellen and Hedwig.

Mr. and Mrs. Henry G. Mueller

Mueller ran a flour mill and box factory. He built a sawmill in company with W. Halbach in 1868, in town of Herman, and they ran the mill together until 1873. Mueller then ran it alone for another two years. He built his flour mill in 1875. He also ran a cheese box factory and manufactured 50,000 boxes per year.

Adolph Bohlman's threshing crew at Henry Mueller's barn. Among those pictured are Bohlman, Mr. Kohl, Ferdinand Schneider and Otto Pieper.

George and Wilhelmina Pieper

The Piepers- George Pieper and his wife, Wilhelmina Garvins Pieper, were early settlers in the Millersville area. George Pieper's name first appears in Sheboygan County on a deed in a land transaction where he is listed as holding the mortgage when Charles Sprung (sic) (Sprenger) bought land from Ludvig Karstaedt, dated 1857. George Pieper owned much of the land in the Millersville area and brother, August, owned land in the north Howards Grove area. Two other brothers moved to Minnesota. Many of the subdivisions in Millersville are on land once owned by the Pieper family- Country Aire, Cardinal Heights, most of Stonebridge and land along Alcott Avenue and Millersville Avenue.

Image from the 1875 Sheboygan County Atlas showing a drawing of the residence of Millersville area resident George Pieper, Section 26, Town of Herman, Today the land that was part of the farm is located on Alcott Avenue, the street leading to the Howards Grover sanitary sewer plant. The house located there now was built after fire destroyed the one pictured here.

Above is a photo taken at the 50th anniversary celebration of George and Wilhelmina Garvins Pieper in their barn about 1906. Herman (1) and Anna Sprenger (2) can be seen in the center. Arwin Sprenger (3) is seated at the right front.

Memories by Arline Sprenger Hoppe

When I was a teenager my grandmother, Anna Sprenger Pieper (nee Hammelmann) also known as Oma, told me about her parents coming to the United States. Her father August Hammelmann and Justine Strassburg were married in Germany in 1863. They lived in a small community in the Brandenburg Province, Germany near Prenzlau. An uncle and aunt, the Alex Harps, had come to the U.S. in 1854 and lived about two miles west of Millersville.

So in 1866 the Hammelmanns came on a steamboat with other German immigrants landing at the Port of New York after being on the water for three weeks. They then traveled from New York to Sheboygan on a train and on the Great Lakes.

When they arrived in Sheboygan they had only $2.50 to their name. From Sheboygan to Town Herman they traveled by oxen. When the oxen came to a river, they didn't go over the log bridge, but through the water. All their clothes and trunk contents got wet. They then walked the last four miles. Her mother, Justine, was so homesick for Germany that she sat down and cried. The $2.50 they had, they loaned to a friend, so they arrived penniless at their Uncle and Aunt's home.

They worked at various farms and saw mills in Manitowoc and Sheboygan Counties, then eventually bought a farm about two miles north of Howards Grove and lived there for thirteen years, later moving back to Howards Grove.

They had eight children; two died in Germany and one died here in infancy. After her mother died in 1912, her father, August Hammelmann, lived with my grandmother, Oma Pieper in Millersville. He died in 1920 at age 84.

W. and Mrs. Sprenger

An article in the 1953 *Sheboygan Press* stated that Millersville had a population of 260 people living in 48 homes, 31 people with the name of Sprenger. According to the Germans to America research series, there were many Sprungs listed immigrating to America starting around 1852.

Evidently the Sprung name was changed to Sprenger as the St. Paul's Lutheran Church lists a Ferdinand Sprung born June 16, 1861, the son of Karl Sprung and Maria Busch. A deed that was recorded showed Charles Sprung bought 120 acres about a mile west of Millersville for $1,350 from Ludwig Karstedt on June 18, 1857. Of this he had to pay $450 to George Pieper who had a mortgage on the property. This is the area where brothers, Karl and Friedrich Sprenger, bought land and built their homes around 1863.

Karl was married to Christina Winter and Friedrich to Friedricka Winter. I was told that some of the Sprengers that left Germany went to South Africa and Argentina in South America. These are pictures of W. Sprenger and wife taken in Kingwilliamstown, Cape of Good Hope, South Africa.

A son of Friedrich Sprenger, Herman, owned a store in Howards Grove in the 1890s dealing in dry goods, notions, groceries, wine, liquors and cigars.

In 1890 he purchased the mill from Henry Mueller in Millersville.

The Karstedt's

Johann Ludwig Karstedt II and his wife Louise Boethke came to America in August of 1855 with their children. They settled on a farm in Sheboygan County, Herman Township, Section 26, the S ½ of the NE ¼. This plot of land was obtained from the United States government by Christian Weike in 1846 and then sold to a Ludwick Karl or Karl Ludwick in 1850. The Karstedt's purchased the land on November 19, 1855.

Their second child, Johann Ludwig Karstedt III served in the Civil War and is buried in Howards Grove. Their third child, Gottlieb Frederick Karstedt enlisted into the military in Town Herman and served in the Civil War from August 21, 1862 to August 29, 1865. Johann and Louise's fourth child, Karl Frederick Wilhelm Karstedt, also known as Charles, operated a blacksmith shop in Howards Grove. The seventh child of Johann and Louise, Herman Albert Karstedt started a saddlery business in Howards Grove. Herman and his brother, Karl, later moved to Minneapolis, Minnesota. The ninth child, Albert Karl Emil Karstedt and his wife, Lena Meyer, purchased the 80 acre farm from Ludwig and Louise on December 5, 1882. They had eight children, Paul, Walter, Lillie, Selma, Alma, Louis, Albert and Emmanuel. On October 21, 1916 Walter and his wife Elsie Kaestner purchased the farm from Albert. They had one son, Harold. Harold and Marion Roehl purchased the farm from Walter on January 2, 1947.

Harold and Marion retired from farming in 1981 and built a new house next to the farmhouse. Parcels of land were sold over approximately 20 years for business and residential development. And so ended the 126 years of farming for the Karstedt family.

The Karstedt farmhouse is located at 607 South Wisconsin Drive. The house at 507 South Wisconsin Drive was also part of the homestead. This house was occupied by each of the retired farmers after selling the farm to their sons. The barn was razed in 1991.

The subdivision on this land is called Village View. Businesses which built on the land once owned by the Karstedts are Sheboygan Aurora and Varish Chiropractic Clinics, Lindstrom Dental and the new Cleveland State Bank.

Millersville School

Millersville School, 1906

The first free school in the town of Herman was established in 1848 by E.W. Schlichting. Built of logs, it was known as the District #1 school.

The first teacher was Miss Eva Atwood from Sheboygan Falls. She taught for five or six months each school term, and was paid $32 per month for her services. School was held in an addition of the Charles Oetling farm house in Millersville which was located in the northwest corner of Highway 32 and Millersville Avenue. The house still stands there and is the residence of Carl Herzog, great grandson of Charles.

In 1868, a separate school building was built across the street at a cost of $355 paid to Carl Bohlman for construction costs. Some remodeling took place in 1927. Bathroom facilities were added in the 1940s.

The 1948 Sheboygan County Superintendent's Report stated that the large enrollment of the school made necessary the change from a rural to a state graded school. This meant the addition of another school room and a second teacher. The new room was finally added during the 1951-52 school year. Used for the four upper grades, the original schoolroom was remodeled and used for the primary grades. During the 1953-54 school year the school had 57 students enrolled.

Following the consolidation of school districts in 1959 the school continued to operate as an elementary school and remained open until 1972. The building was used as the village hall for many years.

Millersville School Teachers 1848-1972

	YEAR		YEAR
Miss Elva Atwood	1848	Carol Mueller, Prin.	
Miss E.L. Crosby	1868-71	Grace Helmer	1948-50
Miss M. Mitchell	1872	Judith Puls Schlehlein	
Miss Helen Richardson	1873	Grace Helmer	1950-51
Miss E.L. Crosby	1874	Judith Puls Schlehlein	
Gilbert Gillman	1875-76	Carol Mueller	
Mary Thomas	1877	Grace Helmer	1951-52
Miss E.L. Crosby	1878-80	Laverne Hildebrand	
Miss Ellen Weeks	1881	Judith Schehlein	
Miss Maggie Mitchell	1882-85	Gerald Saemann	1952-53
Miss Mary Marten	1886	Laverne Hildebrand	
Hannah Brink	1887-89	Gerald Saemann	1953-54
Adelia Hillman	1890	Elizabeth Kranendonk	
Alma Joems	1891	Gerald Saemann	1954-55
T. Kuhlmey	1892	Eleanor Bub	
W. Strassburger	1893-94	Caroline Moenning	1955-56
A.O. Heuer	1895-96	Eleanor Bub	
A.O. Heuer	1897-98	Evelyn Koene	1956-57
Gust Dexheimer	1899-1900	Eleanor Bub	
Elsie Sebald	1901-02	Evelyn Koene	1957-59
Charles Joch	1903-04	Jeannette Kuhlow	
Daisy George	1905-06	Evelyn Koene	1959-66
Alma Habighorst	1907-11	Kathryn Maercklein	
Elsa Voet	1911-12	Evelyn Koene	1966-67
Adele Bein	1912-16	Rosemarie (Krier) Abts	
Norma Frome	1919-19	Elmer Koppelmann	1967-68
Valeska Gersmehl	1919-20	Rosemarie (Krier) Abts Mary (Bramstedt) Roerdink	1967-69
Norma Frome	1920-21		
Otto Schomberg	1921-23	Rosemarie (Krier) Abts Mary (Bramstedt) Roerdink	1969-71
Carl Luth	1923-24		
Florence Herman	1924-25	Lorraine Sperhake	
Evelyn Trossen	1925-27	Jeanelle Bennin	1971-72
Lucille Harkins	1927-29	Lorraine Sperhake	
Marie Zuengler	1929-36		
Violet Herberg	1936-44		
Ruth Fenner	1944-46		
Grace Helmer	1946-48		

Millersville School
1908

Bottom Row: Meta Nix Bock, Anne Goedeke Bramstedt, Ada Prigge Mauer, Friedola Kohl Bodenstab, Viola Usadel Herzog, Edna Pieper Bohlmann, Arthur Usadel, John Prigge, Walter Pieper, Albert Karstedt, Ziegfried Lallemant, Walter Mueller, Gustav Nagel, Immanuel Karstedt, John Goedeke

2nd Row: Emma Goedeke Cone, Little Boy

3rd Row: Helen Nix Feldmann, Helen Nagel, Martha Lallemant, Esther Nagel, Edna Goedeke Johne, Viola Mueller Kohl, Arwin Sprenger, Arthur Nagel, Louis Karstaedt

4th Row: (Teacher) Laura Habighorst, Hattie Goedeke Roeder, Adele Usadel Erbstoeszer, John Boeldt

Millersville School
1914

1. Harvey Schorer
2. Elmer Kueter
3. Theodore Kohl
4. Henry Mueller
5. Arvin Dickman
6. Arno Nix
7. Ervin Prange
8. Erwin Mielke
9. Harvey Sprenger
10. Walter Rau
11. George Wuestenhagen
12. Mabel Kueter (Schneider)
13. Linda DeKarsky (Pieper)
14. Leona Dengel (Schomberg)
15. Leona Henning (Mueller)
16. Coretta Sprenger (Kohl)
17. Wilma Oetling (Schneider)
18. Elenora Oetling (Herzog)
19. Leona Schorer (Wehrmann)
20. Ella Bohlmann
21. Aurelia Wuestenhagen (Illig)
22. Elsie Berth (Illig)
23. Elnora Kohl
24. Norma Kueter
25. Adela Sprenger (Doro)
26. Frieda Kohl
27. Eleanora Dengel (Nordholz)
28. Louis Bohlmann
29. Harold Sprenger
30. Ella Bitter
31. Mary Dickmann (Boeldt)
32. Leona Kohl
33. Reinhold Sprenger
34. Herman Berth
35. Arthur Heuer
36. Adela Bein (Teacher)

Millersville School
1922

1st Row: Arno Sprenger, Norman Klein, Frederick Sprenger, Lester Kueter, Marcella Imig

2nd Row: Elva Wuestenhagen, Gertrude Boeldt, Norma Duerwaechter, Alice Goedeke, Verona Goedeke, Norma Dengel, Florence Boeldt, Gertrude Prigge, Gordon Wuestenhagen, Arthur Bennin, Hugo Wuestenhagen, Herbert Sohn, Milton Wiedemeyer

3rd Row: Harvey Bennin, Elmer Kueter, Corita Sprenger, Aurelia Heuer, Roma Schorer, Pearl Horneck, Henry Bennin, Lorraine Pieper, Milford Henning, Harvey Schorer, Elmer Imig, Gerhard Prigge, Norma Oetling, Cyril Horneck

4th Row: Lydia Wiedemeyer, Elnora Oetling, Leona Dengel, Leona Henning, Norbert Mielke, Wilma Oetling, (Teacher) Otto Schomberg

Millersville School
1933

Front Row: Elaine Herzog Rautmann, Marcella Neumann Boedeker, Margaret Bitter Zuege, Evelyn Heusterberg Sprenger, Roger Doro, La Vern Herzog Schueffner, Eunice Schneider Dirks, Adela Heusterberg Damrow, Benita Heuer Bitter, Irma Pieper Reseburg, Ernest Illig, Marvin Gabrielse, Robert Kuether, William Prigge, Raymond Bitter

2nd Row: ____, Hubert Dengel, Harold Bitter, Norman Scheibl, ____, Mabel Sprenger Janke, Ellen Scheibl Wilhel, Mildred Klein Fenn, Ruby Heusterberg Schomberg, Doris Kuether Fischer, Elroy Grunewald, Lawrence Gabrielse, ? Sally Gabrielse, Richard Kuether, Elton Kalk, ____, Zerlina Imig Melger

3rd Row: Doris Sprenger Ringel, Florence Kohl Hildebrand, Friedola Dengel, Elvera Bohlmann Kohl, Armond Kueter, Willard Scheibl, Harold Karstedt, George Sprenger, Sophie Pieper Kuhn, Rose Boeldt Sprenger, Cora Kalk Kleinhaus, Elizabeth Gabrielse, Ernst Pieper, Elmer Pieper, Bernice Sprenger Thomson, Verna Heusterberg Groene, Ruth Kuether Fischer

Not listed on picture: William Imig, Elmer Bitter, Dorothy Bitter, Lester Sprenger, Dorothy Wuestenhagen.

Millersville School
1934

Front Row: Roger Doro, Ernest Illig , Carl Sprenger, Robert Mueller, William Prigge, Lester Sprenger, Norman Scheibl, Harold Bitter, James Doro, Harold Imig, Arwin Herzog Jr.

2nd Row: Elaine Heuer, Arline Sprenger, Marvin Gabrielse, Irma Pieper, Delores Wuestenhagen, Elaine Herzog, Marion Herzog, Raymond Bitter, Betty Jane Klemme, Mirtha Heuer, Evelyn Heusterberg, La Vern Herzog

3rd Row: Marcella Neumann, Adela Heusterberg, Marcella Gabrielse, Benita Heuer, Mildred Klein, Zerlina Imig, Mabel Sprenger, Ruth Bitter, Margaret Bitter, Bernetta Illig, Doris Oetling

4th Row: Ruby Heusterberg, Elmer Pieper, Dorothy Bitter, Ernst Pieper, Elvera Bohlmann, Leonard Gabrielse, Doris Sprenger, Elroy Grunewald, Ellen Scheibl, Elmer Bitter, (Teacher) Marie Zuengler Harms

Millersville School
1936

Front Row: Shirley Larson, Evelyn Heusterberg, Tony Severson, Margaret Bitter, William Prigge

2nd Row: Elaine Herzog, Ruth Bitter, Jane Herzog, Ernest Illig, Dorothy Severson, Roger Doro, Raymond Bitter, Adela Heusterberg

3rd Row: Douglas Severson, Arwin Herzog, Delores Klemme Jeanette Illig, Elaine Heuer, Donald Bitter, Benita Heuer, Robert Severson, Bernetta Illig

4th Row: Raymond Wuestenhagen, Severson, Alfred Bitter Jr., Marion Herzog, Roger Wuestenhagen, Sally Gabrielse, Marvin Gabrielse

5th Row: Carl Sprenger, Delores Wuestenhagen, Mirtha Heuer, Severson, Arline Sprenger, Robert Mueller, Betty Klemme, Marcella Neumann

6th Row: James Doro, Harold Imig, Irma Pieper, La Vern Herzog, Zerlina Imig, Eunice Schneider, Doris Oetling, Lester Sprenger, (Teacher) Miss Violet Herberg

Millersville School
1939

Top Row: Doris Oetling, Irma Pieper, Roger Doro, Evelyn Heusterberg, James Doro, Eunice Schneider, Ernst Illig, Elaine Herzog, Myrtle Schneider

2nd Row: Orville Knoener, Karl Sprenger, Robert Mueller, Henry Boeldt, Marion Herzog, Howard Boeldt, Jane Herzog, Raymond Bitter, Elaine Heuer

3rd Row: Arline Sprenger, Mirtha Heuer, Donald Bitter, Alfred Bitter Jr., Joyce Beinemann, Kenneth Beinemann, Allene Kaemmer, Arwin Herzog Jr., Jeanette Illig

4th Row: Charlotte Beinemann, Edward Mueller, Eldora Boeldt, Margaret Illig, Marie Bitter, Norma Wuestenhagen, Gladys Harms, Carl Mueller, Carol Mae Klein

5th Row: Shirley Herzog, Caroline Sprenger, (Teacher) Violet Herberg

In 1951-52 school term a new addition was added to the school and the old classroom was remodeled. These are pictures of the inside of the newly remodeled school in 1953.

(New classroom upper grades)

Row 1: Alan Harms, Ellwyn Aschenbach, Steve Sprenger, Darryl Aschenbach, Robert Bitter, Eugene Sebald
Row 2: Deanna Fenn, Carol Jean Schneider, Jerome Sprenger, Carl Harms, Helen Henning, Sharon Sprenger
Row 3: ___, Marlee Gabrielse, Thomas Usadel, Carl Herzog
Row 4: Mary Harms, Earl Goedeke, ___, John Henning

(Remodeled classroom upstairs lower grades)

Row 1: Gloria Hoppe, Shirley Reseburg, Joann Schneider, Judy Wuestenhagen

Row 2: John Harms, John Sprenger, Nancy Gabrielse, Diane Schneider, Lynne Usadel

Row 3: ___, ___, ___, Joan Wiedemeyer, ___,

Row 4: Mary Wiedemeyer, Judy Harms, Judy Kuester, Judy Goedeke

Millersville School
1951 - 1952
Grades 5 to 8

Front Row: John Henning, Jerome Sprenger, La Vern Harms, Diane Mercer, Carl Herzog, Carl John Harms

2nd Row: Deanna Fenn, Marlee Gabrielse, Mary Harms, Helen Henning, Carol Rau, Sharon Sprenger, Leonard Gabrielse, Thomas Usadel, Carol Jean Schneider

3rd Row: Janet Harms, Joyce Schorer, Earl Goedeke, Barbara Gabrielse, Pat Sprenger, Eileen Schneider, Karl Hoppe, Virginia Hoppe, (Teacher) Grace Helmer

Millersville School

1951 – 1952

Grades 1 to 4

Front Row: John Sprenger, James Gabrielse, Jerome Schomberg, Eugene Herzog

2nd Row: Dianne Schneider, Nancy Gabrielse, Gloria Hoppe, Joan Schneider, Joanne Schneider, Lynn Usadel

3rd Row: Michael Hildebrand, Janet Bitter, Annabelle Kohl, Joanne Hoppe, Alan Harms, Judith Wuestenhagen, Glenn Mueller

4th Row: Mary Wiedemeyer, Barbara Klein, David Kohl, Eugene Sebald, Robert Bitter, Ellwyn Aschenbach, Darryl Aschenbach, (Teacher) Laverne Hildebrand

Millersville School
1952 – 1953
Upper Grades

Front Row: Alan Harms, Steve Sprenger, Robert Bitter, John Henning, Carl John Harms, Darryl Aschenach, Ellwyn Aschenbach

2nd Row: Eugene Sebald, Carl Herzog, Diane Mercer, Mary Harms, Marlee Gabrielse, James Laack, La Vern Harms, Jerome Sprenger, Carol Jean Schneider

3rd Row: (Teacher) Gerald Saemann, Joyce Schorer, Sharon Sprenger, Karl Hoppe, Eileen Schneider, Earl Goedeke, Virgina Hoppe, Helen Henning, Deanna Fenn, Thomas Usadel

Millersville School

1954 – 1955

Grades 1 - 4

Front Row: Donald Herzog, Gene Kueter, John Harms, Eugene Herzog, Richard Pieper

2nd Row: Christine Goedeke, Jo Ann Bitter, Sandra Wagner, Karen Kuhn, Karen Herzog, Joan Sprenger, Janice Reseburg, Rita Usadel

3rd Row: Shirley Reseburg, Marilyn Sprenger, Lynn Heuer, Alan Sprenger, Lee Schomberg, Joan Schneider, John Sprenger, Mary Kohl, Ervin Hoppe, Dianne Schneider, Joan Wiedemeyer

4th Row: Practice teacher, Eileen Meinnert, Gloria Hoppe, Judy Goedeke, Judy Wuestenhagen, Annabelle Kohl, Nancy Gabrielse, Lynne Usadel, Jo Ann Schneider, Janice Grunewald, (Teacher) Mrs. Bub

Millersville School
1955 -1956
1 to 4

Top Row: Mrs. Eleanor Bub, Dale Voss, Lynn Heuer, Connie Heiling, Joan Wiedemeyer, Larry Boggs, Janice Gruenewald, Marilyn Sprenger, Karen Kuhn

2nd Row: Donald Herzog, Gene Kueter, Ervin Hoppe, Alan Sprenger, Christine Goedeke, Ronnie Schomberg, David Meinhardt, Nancy Kalk, Connie Boggs

3rd Row: Arthur Kessler, Carol Karstedt, Janice Reseburg, David Heiling, Dale Sprenger, Janice Hoppe, Richard Pieper, Jo Ann Bitter, Rita Usadel

4th Row: Joan Sprenger, Sandra Wagner, Eilleen Meinhardt, Roy Henning, James Kultgen, Billy Kohl

Millersville School
1957 - 1958

Top Row: (Teacher) Jeanette Kuhlow, Linda Valenstein, Art Kessler, Janice Reseburg, Donald Herzog, Ronald Schomberg, William Kohl, Carol Karstedt

2nd Row: Tom Kohl, Judy Sprenger, Roy Henning, Janice Hoppe

3rd Row: David Goetsch, Mary Kueter, Nancy Kalk, James Kultgen

4th Row: Molly Harms, Diane Reseburg, Dale Sprenger, Lynn Boedecker

5th Row: Gwen Becker, Susan Valenstein, Faye Usadel, Mary Goetsch, Kathy Gabrielse, Carol Bitter, Sandy Hoppe

Millersville School
1959 – 1960
Upper Grades

1st Row: Roy Henning, Christine Goedeke, William Kohl, Rita Usadel, Gene Kueter, Joan Sprenger

2nd Row: James Kultgen, Janice Reseburg, Linda Valenstein, Arthur Kessler, Janice Hoppe, Sandra Wagner

Standing: Lynn Heuer, Paul Burkhardt, Joan Wiedemeyer, Alan Sprenger, Marilyn Sprenger, Ervin Hoppe, Jo Ann Bitter, Richard Pieper, Janice Grunewald, Karen Kuhn, Dale Sprenger, Donald Herzog

MILLERSVILLE
GRADE SCHOOL
1962-1963
Upper room

Top Row: Paula Valenstein, David Wehrmann, Gene Spindler, Sandy Harms

2nd Row: Susan Valenstein, Mark Bitter, Carol Bitter, Alan Reseburg, Sandy Hoppe

3rd Row: Richard Kuether, Faye Usadel, Richard Merkel, Marilyn Kultgen, Dennis Sprenger

4th Row: Daniel Kuether, Becky Juroff, Laura Kimme, Gene Feldmann, Tim Juroff

Millersville School
1965-66
Grades 1-2-3

Top Row: Galan Feldman, Lori Augustine, Daniel Wehrmann, Brenda Kumbalek, Alan Kuether, Nancy Schneider, Dean Sommer, Karen Koeser, Rusty Augustine

2nd Row: Beth Kuether, Joy Debbink, Emily Mattson, Cheryl Juroff, Nancy Klingeisen, Lisa Kumbalek, Susan Hoppe, Ruth Chasteen

3rd Row: Mrs. Maercklein, Tommy Beck, Debbie Wichmann, Randy Bitter, Ruth Grunewald, Jerry Wehrmann, Debbie Pieper, Patty Wehrmann, Tommy Schneider

Millersville School

1966-67

Grades 1 & 2

Top Row: Bobby Schloss, Viginia Kimme, Lisa Kumbalek, Cindy Wuestenhagen, Barbara Miller, Jerry Wehrmann, Emily Mattson, Randy Bitter, Nancy Klingeisen

2nd Row: Donna Kumbalek, Cheryl Loersch, Vicky Sandvig, Susan Schueler, JC DoBas

3rd Row: Miss Krier, David Schloss, Joy Debbink, Allen Goddard, Sandy Spindler, Tommy Haack, Donna Grunewald, Brian Koeser, Cheryl Juroff

Millersville School
1967-68
Grades 3-5

Top Row: Mr. Koppelmann, Lori Augustine, Rusty Augustine, Lisa Kumbalek, Steve DoBas, Brenda Kumbalek, Galan Feldmann

2nd Row: Dean Sommer, Ruth Grunewald, Rene Badtke, Alan Kuether

3rd Row: Susan Hoppe, Bobby Schloss, Cheryl Juroff, Nancy Klingeisen, Arthur Nelson, Kim Brendel

4th Row: Tommy Schneider, Nancy Schneider, Joy Debbink. Karen Koeser, Debbie Pieper, Randy Bitter

5th Row: Tommy Beck, Beth Kuether, Jerry Wehrmann, Kay Kallas, Emily Mattson, Debbie Wickmann, Barbara Miller

Millersville School

1968-69

Grades 3 & 4

Top Row: Barb Miller, Jerry Wehrmann, Joy Debbink, David Schloss, Kay Kallas, Bobby Schloss, Miss Bramstedt

2nd Row: Randy Bitter, Cheryl Juroff, Emily Mattson, Tommy Beck

3rd Row: Lisa Kumbalek, Barb Reese

4th Row: JC DoBas, Donna Grunewald, Brian Koeser, Tommy Haack, Cheryl Loersch, Arthur Nelson

5th Row: Virginia Kimme, Susan Schueler, Nancy Klingeisen, Vicki Sandvig, Donna Kumbalek, Sandy Spindler, Cindy Wuestenhagen

School Activities

January 31, 1935

Friday was visiting day for mothers at the local school here, and many mothers and friends of the district were the honored guests at the afternoon classes and society meeting of the school. A very interesting program planned by the fifth grade pupils was enjoyed by all. The program was announced by Margaret Bitter:

Ten Little Brownies-Ruth Bitter and the first and second grade pupils

A Recitation: *Where Are You Going My Little Cat?*- Elaine Herzog

The Old Spinning Wheel-A harmonica selection by the Harmonica Club

Playing Store- Benita Heuer and Evelyn Heusterberg

Hundreds of Stars- Irma Pieper

The Dandelion- Evelyn Heusterberg and Mirtha Heuer

Mother- A song by the fifth grade

The Wind and the Sun- Roger Doro, Ernest Illig and Marvin Gabrielse

Guitar and Harmonica Selections- Ruby Heusterberg

Whisky-Frisky-Doris Oetling

Buy My Toys-Elaine Heuer

The Snowflakes-Second Grade

Aunt Doleful's Ailments-Sixth Grade

Songs-Seventh and Eighth Grades

The World is Full of a Number of Things-Delores Wuestenhagen

Millersville

Mrs. A.E. Kaemmer

R.1 Sheboygan, Wis.

Sheboygan County News

May 24, 1937

The Millersville School gave a program at Otto Sprenger's hall on Tuesday evening which was as follows: Rhythm Band and songs- First and Second Grades; Songs by Allene Kaemmer; *Mrs. Brown's Visitors*- A dialogue by five pupils; Piano Accordion Music by Bernetta Illig; Rhythm Band; Piano Accordion Music-by Eunice Schneider; Group Singing; Duet, *Whispering Hopes*, *By the Old Mill Stream*-Adela Huesterberg and Sally Gabrielse; *Toy Town Admiral*-A drill by 10 children; Play, *Who's The Boss?*- by nine 7th and 8th graders.

Millersville
Mrs. A.E. Kaemmer
R.1 Sheboygan, Wis.
Sheboygan County News
May 23, 1938

Quite a few from this village attended the operetta given by the Howards Grove High school Tuesday evening at the community hall at Howards Grove. Those from this district who took part were the Misses LaVerne Herzog, Bernetta Illig, Adela Heusterberg, Ruby Heusterberg and Doris Strassburger.

The Millersville school children gave a program at Al Doro's hall on Wednesday evening which was largely attended. The program was as follows: Welcome by Allene Kaemmer; rhythm band by grades 3-8, director, Evelyn Heusterberg; drill, The Modern School by the kindergarten, first and second grades; a speech by Junior Bitter; song and dance by eight girls; piano accordion selections by Eunice Schneider, Orville Knoener and Roger Doro; group singing by grades 3-8; play, *Rats* by the 8th grade, characters, Mr. Whiffle-William Prigge, Mrs. Whiffle-Marcella Neumann, Mrs. Penny-Margaret Bitter, Uncle Peter-Marvin Gabrielse; string music, James Doro and Betty Jane Klemme-guitars- and Donald Bitter-violin- Miss Violet Herberg, the teacher, directed the program.

Sheboygan County News
December 27, 1938

The Millersville School, under the direction of their teacher, Miss Violet Heberg, presented a very interesting program at Al Doro's hall on Monday evening. A large crowd attended. The program was as follows: Opening song, *We're Ready to Begin*; welcome, recitation by Margaret Illeg; drill, *The Little Tin Soldier and the French Doll*, by the primary grades; *Hats*, recitation by three pupils of the kindergarten; instrumental music, James Doro and Donald Bitter; *Santa's Helpers* recitation by two boys; *At the Photographers*, a dialogue; rhythm band directed by Evelyn Heusterberg; *A Strange Difference*, recitation by Allene Kaemmer; *A Minister's Mistake*, a dialogue; song, *Away in Old Judea*; piano accordion selections, by Eunice Schneider; *That Troublesome Christmas Present*, dialogue; *Goodnight*, recitation by Roger Wuestenhagen.

March 1940

The comedy-drama, *Too Good to Miss*, presented Saturday and Sunday evenings at the Monterey Hall, Howards Grove by the Junior Advancement Association, was largely attended. The play was coached by Miss Olinda Prange, Howards Grove, with the Misses Bernice Sprenger, Verna and Ruby Heusterberg and Karl Bohlman of this village and vicinity taking part. Many from here were in attendance.

April 11, 1940

The Millersville Parent-Teachers' association held their monthly meeting at the school on Wednesday evening. It was decided to donate $50 for the stoker recently installed in the school. After the business session a program of music was enjoyed. Those who took part were Arline Sprenger on her Hawaiian guitar, Eunice Schneider and Roger Doro on piano accordions and James Doro with guitar and song: Prizes at cards were awarded to Mrs. Otto Sprenger and Mrs. Otto Schneider. Hostesses were Mrs. Milton Sebald and Mrs. Arwin Sprenger.

Millersville
Mrs. A.E. Kaemmer
R.1 Sheboygan, Wis.
Sheboygan County News

April 29, 1940

The Millersville school pupils are enjoying baseball. On Wednesday afternoon they defeated the Prange School players by a score of 13 to 6 and on Thursday afternoon they added another victory by a score of 8-0 with the Erdman School. Pitcher for the nine is James Doro and catcher is Karl Sprenger. The line-up consists of James and Roger Doro, Karl Sprenger, Ernie Illig, Howard Boeldt, Raymond Bitter Jr., Donald Bitter, Doris Oetling, Marion Herzog, Eunice Schneider and Arline Sprenger. Mr. Erwin Beineman accompanied them as umpire.

Millersville
Mrs. A.E. Kaemmer
R.1 Sheboygan, Wis.
Sheboygan County News
December 19, 1940

The Millersville Parent-Teachers' association held their December meeting at the school on Wednesday evening in the form of a Christmas party. Husbands of the members were the honored guests. During the business session a petition was drawn and sent to the county board for safeguarding the children when crossing at the school on Highway 42. A delightful program was presented by the members after the business meeting which consisted of short plays, duets, quartettes, groups and assembly singing and monologues as follows: 1. Assorted tunes, 2. *Back Numbers* a play given by Miss Elsa Kruse, Mrs. Harvey Sprenger, Mrs. Ervin Beinemann, Mrs. Walter Mueller, Mrs. Walter Schneider, Miss Violet Herberg and Mrs. Otto Sprenger, 3. Duets by Mrs. Rudolph Schorer and Mrs. Otto Sprenger, 4. *A Christmas Disappointment*, a play by Mrs. William Thierfelder and Mrs. Martin Boeldt, 5. *Fruit Cake Recipe*, a play by Mrs. William Thierfelder, Mrs. Arwin Sprenger, Mrs. Walter Schneider and Mrs. Alfred Doro. 7. *It Won't Be Long*, a short sketch by Mrs. Clarence Illig and Mrs. Robert Goedecke, 8. *Father's Joy Ride*, a monologue by Miss Violet Herberg, 9. *Last Year's Letter*, a play by Mrs. Adolph Kaemmer.

Farewell Party Held Wednesday At Millersville
1944

Members of the Millersville Parent-Teacher association, their husbands and children met at the school house on Wednesday evening, and combined their April meeting with a farewell party honoring the children's teacher, Miss Violet Herberg, Sheboygan Falls.

During the business session it was decided to sponsor a public card party at Al Doro's hall in the latter part of April in order to increase funds used for school purposes. The association recently contributed to the Red Cross fund and bond drive. The next meeting will be held on May 3, when election of officers will take place. The hostesses will be Mrs. William Prigge and Mrs. Milton Sebald.

Following the discussion, the party honoring Miss Herberg began. After eight years of teaching in Millersville, she is leaving in May for Wauwatosa, where she has enlisted as a nursing cadet. She was remembered with a gift and a song composed by one of the members and dedicated to her was sung.

The evening was spent at cards with awards merited by Mrs. Harvey Sprenger, Mrs. Arthur Heuer, Arwin Herzog, Miss Hilda Schneider, Mrs. Henry Mueller Jr., Mrs. William Prigge and Mrs. Albert Oetling at sheepshead and by Harvey Harms and Walter Schneider at skat. Later refreshments brought by the members were served to about 75 guests. Hostesses for the party were the official committee, Mrs. William Thiefelder, Mrs. Walter Mueller, Mrs. Milton Sebald and Miss Elsa Kruse.

Annual Meeting of School District # 1, Town of Herman
July 14, 1958

1. The annual meeting of School District Jt. #1 of the Town of Herman and Sheboygan Falls was called to order by the director, Lester Sprenger.

2. The minutes, financial report and the auditing committee report were read by the clerk and accepted.

3. It was decided to paint the entire school building on the outside.

4. Following the reading of recommendations of the county superintendent of schools, a motion was made, seconded and carried to delegate the school board to take care of these matters.

5. It was moved to table purchase of another radio-record player until the board had an opportunity to confer with the teachers and supervisors. Also tabled was the matter of installing a telephone.

6. The school board was asked to hire a janitor for the coming year.

7. The tax levy was set at $11,000 with provision giving the board authority to make short term loans.

8. By motion of the members, the milk program will be continued and board salaries are to remain unchanged.

9. Reuben Hoppe was elected director for a three year term and Fred Boedecker was named to the auditing committee for three years.

10. School was scheduled to start September 2, 1958.

11. The meeting went on record in favor of the township school petition.

Children's pictures are to be taken every three years, except by permission of the school board.

Roland Schomberg, Clerk

Millersville School in 1978- Children raising the flag on a breezy winter morning. Back row left to right: Mary Roerdink, teacher; Wanda Kumbalek, Ann Kallas, Ruth Valenstein, Mike Badtke. Front row, left to right: Deb Prange, Sue Spindler, Marie Schneider, Glenda Feldmann, Colleen Burke, Ken DoBas and Jodi Beck.

St. Paul's Evangelical Lutheran Church of Howards Grove

From the beginning this small country church was known as St. Paul's Evangelical Church of Millersville, but when Millersville and Howards Grove were incorporated in 1967, the church lost that identity. Following is a brief history of the congregation.

Early church services for St. Paul's Lutheran and St. Luke's Lutheran Churches were held in the Mahler School on the Schnaapsville Road (Hwy County J) and the Millersville School. Members soon felt the need of a cemetery and started one next to the Mahler School. This cemetery can still be seen on County Hwy J, ¼ mile west of Hwy 32. In the early years pastors traveled through dense forests to minister to the needs of these early German settlers. A Pastor Erbe of the Reformed Church held services in these schools. However, since many of these people were of Lutheran heritage, it was with great joy that they welcomed the first Lutheran missionary, the Rev. Johann Sprengling, a member of the Wisconsin Synod who was serving St. Peter's Lutheran Church in Town Mosel (Haven). Through his efforts St. Paul's Church of Town Herman and St. Luke's of the Town of Sheboygan Falls came into being.

This pastor organized St. Paul's Congregation in 1862, and immediately plans were made for a church building, 20 x 26 feet, which was dedicated in 1863. The oldest document in the possession of St. Paul's is the warranty deed of the real estate on the corner of Highway 32 and Playbird Road, dated February 13, 1865, which was donated by Mr. and Mrs. Gottleib Kuck. On January 10, 1867 St. Paul's was incorporated, signed by the following: Carl Bohlmann, George Pieper, Friedrich Meves, Michael Schwalbe, Michel Huhs, Wilhelm Kleinhans, Karl Monnich, Christian Wolter, Christian Bennin, W. Bennin, W. Heuer, Christian Strassburger, Carl Henning, Friedrich Sprenger, Carl Sprenger, Heinrich Roll, C. Rahn, C. Ziemke, Conrad Schomberg, Gotttlieb Kuch, Friedrich Wenthe, Johann Dengel, Carl Liebzeit, Christian Fedler, Friedrich Goedeke, C. Mueller, Johannes Kohl, Wilhelm Luehring and Gottlieb Jochmann.

The first minutes are dated January 3, 1873 and in 1874 the minutes showed St. Paul's possessed a large piece of land. Trustees were elected to supervise church matters and also the farm. It was noted that our forefathers made such diligent use of the church that the floor had to be replaced after 12 years. In 1870 the first resident pastor was the Rev. August Kleinhans, and a parsonage was provided for him. At that time St. Luke Lutheran became a subcharge of St. Paul's. This arrangement prevailed until 1908 when St. Luke severed relations with St. Paul's and the Wisconsin Synod.

Among the first to serve on the church council were Gottlieb Kuck, C. Henning, H. Mahler, F. Ruhlow, Fr. Meves, George Pieper and H. Kohl.

In 1884 a larger church, 36 feet wide and 56 feet long and 21 feet high, was erected at a cost of $4000 on the old cemetery lot. Everyone possessing a team of horses was asked to furnish two loads of stones for the foundation. The building itself was of brick, with arched windows; a new pipe organ and bell were installed. Dedication took place on October 26, 1884. The first renovation was made in 1902 when art glass windows were installed. The cost of the windows was $498 and was a gift from

Congregation Timeline

1862- St. Paul's was officially founded.

1884- A new brick structure, located on the northeast corner of Hwy. 32 and Playbird Road, was built replacing the original structure.

1891- The current cemetery site on Playbird west of Hwy. 32 was purchased.

1903- The baptismal font was dedicated and a two-story house was dedicated as a parsonage.

1912- 50th anniversary of St. Paul's was celebrated.

1917- Three level educational building was erected. (No longer exists)

1923- First services in English were held. Previously all were given in German. The Ladies' Aid was also organized.

1931- Sunday School and a church choir were started.

1952- The church was remodeled, adding a full basement for a meeting room and kitchen.

1962- 100th anniversary of St. Paul's congregation was celebrated.

1967- Christian education building was dedicated.

1973- Church interior was renovated.

1974- Christian day school began.

1976- Regular services in German were concluded.

1979- New Parsonage on Highway 32 was built.

1984- 100th anniversary of church building on Hwy.32 and Playbird was celebrated.

Henry Ohse. In 1926 an altar and vestry were added to the church. The pointed steeple was replaced by a square one with a battlemented tower rail. This, however, proved impractical and later was replaced again with a pointed steeple in 1939. The organ which had been in the main auditorium was moved to the gallery and the interior was newly decorated and wired for electricity. In 1930 blowers were installed in the organ and furnace of the church. When the iron fencing around the church property was damaged in 1930, it was removed and replaced by cement posts at the driveways and in front of the church and equipped with electric lights. The church was again completely renovated and redecorated in 1952. A 95 foot well was drilled that spring and the entire basement excavated and an addition was built at the back for a kitchen and furnace room with plumbing and heating installed. The balcony was remodeled, a new pipe organ installed and two new stair towers built north and south of the front entrance. New lighting fixtures, new pews and carpeting were installed and the church interior was redecorated. That renovation, completed for the congregation's 90th anniversary, and the dedication of the new pipe organ took place on September 27, 1953. The church was again renovated in 1973. A lowered pine ceiling was installed, carpeting was laid throughout the nave, narthex and choir loft, dark wainscoting was erected with light-colored walls which emphasize the beauty of the stained glass windows and the original altar statue of Christ.

All chancel furnishings, complete sets of Antipendia in all of the liturgical colors are new. The furnishings and appointments were purchased with memorials given in honor of congregation members.

1993- Began use of new Lutheran hymnal.

2001- St. Paul's purchases 20.2 acre property on Millersville Avenue in Howards Grove.

2002- St. Paul's begins building new church and school on Millersville property.

2003- Last services and classes held at old facility. First services and classes held at new facility on Millersville Avenue.

2006- 75th anniversary of St. Paul's Sunday School.

THE SHEBOYGAN PRESS, Tuesday, August 14, 1962

THE OLDEST PICTURE of a confirmation class displayed at the recent centennial of St. Paul's Lutheran Church, Millersville, was this one of the 1895 class. From left, rear, are the Rev. M. H. Hillemann, Anna Marold, Helma Oetling, Julius Fischer, Augusti Bennin, George Quehl, Antone Prange, Albert Usadel, Siedonia Arnoldi, Wilhelm Fuhrman and Lillie Pieper. Front: Pauline Henning, Beanke Winkel, Alma Pieper, Clara Reische, Willie Janke, Ferdinand Kueter and Emil Prange. Another member of the class, Lillie Damrow, is not shown. Four from the class of 18 are living. They are Helma Oetling Dexheimer, Ada; George Quehl, Milwaukee, and Siedonia Arnoldi Gosse and Lillie Pieper Mueller, both of Sheboygan. — (Photo courtesy of George Quehl).

1895 Confirmation Class

St. Paul's Lutheran Church, at left, built in 1884 and located on the northeast corner of Highway 42 later Highway 32 and Playbird Road. The first school, at right, was torn down in 1966.

Christian School-The school was erected in 1917 for $3450. The first to serve on the school board were John Boll, William Prigge and Martin Boeldt. The three-level 30 x 48 foot building consisted of a first floor schoolroom with storage facilities, a second floor meeting hall with a stage and cloakrooms and a full basement with a furnace where mission festival and kinderfest meals were served. Summer school classes in Bible history, catechism and reading and writing in the German language were conducted for grades one through eight for four weeks in June of each year. The school was also the site for confirmation classes, Ladies' Aid, organized in 1923, and Young People's Society, organized in the early 1900s as the Jugendverein and later revived by Reverend Mielke. In 1966 the school was offered to the highest bidder and removed from the premises to make room for the erection of a modern educational building which was dedicated in 1967. In 1974, St. Paul's opened its Christian Day School with grades K through five. St. Paul's joined the Manitowoc Lutheran High School Federation in 1976.

Members being primarily of German origin, services were held in German until 1923, when the first English services were held on a once-every-other-month basis. Gradually most services were held in English, and by 1965 two English services and one German service were held every Sunday. The last German service was held in 1976. The first all English confirmation class was confirmed in 1940. Prior to this there were, at times one or two still confirmed in German with other English confirmands. The *Sheboygan County News* reported on May 9, 1940 that English services were held on the first and third Sundays and German on the second and fourth Sundays.

The year after his arrival in 1930, Pastor Kuether organized the first Sunday school with 70 children, Bible class and a senior choir with 26 members. The lighted ornamental cement posts on the iron fence which surrounded the church and parsonage for many years were a special project of Pastor Kuether. The 75th anniversary of St. Paul's Sunday School was celebrated in 2006. Carl Toepel, in 2006, retired after teaching Sunday School for 50 years. Jane Konik retired in 2008 after teaching for fifty-five years.

Other organizations of the church include: Married Couples Club organized by Pastor Meyer in 1961 and later changed to the Adult Club discontinued in 2000; Altar Guild formed in 1969; Parents-Teachers-Friends (PTF) in 1974; evening Lutheran Ladies League in 1980 and discontinued in 2006; Boys and Girls Pioneers in the early 1990s. The clothing committee has been sorting and packing clothing every fall since the 1970s for Goodwill, Bethesda Resale Shop and Lutheran World Relief. Since 2004, used clothing and other resale items have been given to the Manitowoc Lutheran High School "Repeat Performance" store.

A number of St. Paul's sons and daughters have become ministers, Christian day school teachers or missionaries. The following have entered the ministry: Donald Bitter, A.J. Kunde, Robert Bitter, Thomas Schneider, John Gierach and Mark Bitter. The following entered the field of Christian education: Patricia Sprenger Loersch, Joyce Schorer Krueger, Sharon Sprenger Gutenberger, Marie Meyer Heckmann, Janet Bitter Radue, Marjorie Toepel, Joann Bitter Jurgens, Carol Bitter Weber, Rebecca Juroff Miller, Kathryn Juroff, Cheryl Loersch Strecker, Ruth Simonsberger Wiedoff, Kevin Loersch, Lori Loersch Dahlke, Mark Loersch, Lisa Radue and Dave Reinemann. Edith Schneider Hintz served in the African mission field as a medical missionary for several years.

Dates of Service	Pastors
1862-1866	Rev. Johann Phillip Sprengling
1866-1868	Rev. Johann H. Brockman
1868-1870	Rev. Junker
1870-1878	Rev. August Kleinhans
1878-1898	Rev. G.J. Hillermann
1898-1909	Rev. F. AveLallemont
1909-1930	Rev. L.B. Mielke
1930-1949	Rev. H.A. Kuether
1950-1956	Rev. O.W. Heier
1956-1962	Rev. Henry Meyer
1962-1989	Rev. Henry Juroff
1989-1999	Rev. Jonathan Rossman
2000-2005	Rev. Kristian Taves
2005-Present	Rev. Thomas G. Unke

Principals	
1974-1981	Mr. Theodore Lau
1981-2006	Mr. Theodore Berg
2006-	Mr. Mark Nolte

In 1993 a building committee was formed concerning enlarging the church or building a new facility.

In 1998 it was decided to build a new church and school. St. Paul's purchased 20.2 acres of land on Millersville Avenue and started building the new church and school in 2002. The stained glass win

50th Anniversary of the Congregation

St. Paul's Interior, 1912

dows, two large murals, statue of Jesus above the altar, balcony and chancel pews, old baptismal font and several other items were brought from the old church to the new facility. The last services were held in the old church at Highway 32 and Playbird on June 8, 2003. The new church was dedicated in a special service on June 29, 2003. An open house for the community was held on July 12 and 15, 2003; Laying of the cornerstone was held on September 7, 2003. When the Christian Day School started the 2003-2004 school year in the new facility, enrollment including preschool numbered approximately 60, an increase of 20 from the previous year. The 2007-08 school year numbered 73.

A "Living Nativity" with live animals has been presented outside on the church property the first weekend in December since 2003. The presentation, which involves over 200 people, is given every 20 minutes during three hours each evening. Over 2100 people attended the three-day presentation in 2003 and between 1300-1800 have attended each year since.

Church membership exceeded 500 in 1965 and by 1996 reached 600. Church membership in July 2008 was 725.

The congregation has an active history committee.

Interested persons are able to visit St. Paul's and view the history cabinet. It contains photo albums of confirmation classes, St. Paul's history by Arline Hoppe, binders containing obituaries, weddings, St. Paul's Sunday School and Christian Day School, St. Paul's pastors, anniversary services and Manitowoc Lutheran High School.

50th Anniversary of St. Paul's Church building   1884-1934

Rev. H.A. Kuether at left, Parsonage, seen above.

4-Flower Tulip Garden Grown in Garden at Millersville

May 28, 1940

No doubt tulip growers have raised two flowers on one stem or even three, but how many have grown four on one stem?

Mrs. H.A. Kuether of Millersville has. Her husband, who is pastor of St. Paul's Lutheran Church there, presented the editor of The Press with an exquisite sample of one of the four-flower stems Mrs. Kuether grows in her garden.

It is a beautiful bronze tulip with four flowers growing out of the single stem. Mr. Kuether also brought with him a red tulip with three flowers on one stem and a Yellow with two on a stem.

Mrs. Kuether has a field of over 2,500 tulips. She is a lover of all flowers but takes special pride in her tulips.

Kuether children- Top row: Irene, Ruth, Doris, Richard
Bottom row: Eugene, Robert, Vera, Herman Jr.

Looking north on highway 32. The old school is seen at right front and St. Paul's church at rear.

Recollections of Our Country Church
Roland Schomberg

Though my parents were far from lax in raising their family in a religious manner, it was my grandmother who was the influential force in matters of keeping the faith.

The Sabbath was strictly observed and seldom was labor of any kind allowed to interfere with church attendance. Bad weather and illness were considered legitimate excuses but only when of a serious nature.

During the greater part of the year the trusty Model T provided transportation for the three-mile trip to our rural church. In the dead of winter, however, the bobsled drawn by our team of horses was pressed into service. Upon arrival at the church, the horses were usually unhitched and stabled in a long, wooden horse barn on the church premises.

The horse barn was divided into some thirty partitions or stalls, each complete with a separate feed box for each horse. Each horse was secured with a rope after its bit had been removed from its mouth, and small portions of grain stashed away on the buggy or sled were deposited in the box for the animal's munching pleasure. Since a variety of nervous horses were in attendance in unfamiliar surroundings, inevitably there was biting and kicking even though the barns had dividers that were intended to minimize problems.

Our house of worship at St. Paul's Lutheran in the town of Herman, was of typical country church construction – the tall pointed spire, the stained glass windows, the arched main doorway and the high-ceilinged nave. Being built in 1884, the basement was largely unexcavated, but by the time I first attended church in the 1920s, a pipeless furnace had already been installed. Heating the church was the responsibility of the faithful sexton. Depending on the severity of the cold, numerous trips each Sunday morning were necessary to start the wood fire and check it to assure the church-goers of the comfort they expected. In later years he was provided with a quantity of coal to help in the regulation of the fire for more sustained heat.

In addition to this assignment, the sexton also was chief bellringer for the congregation. Not only was the bell rung at church time, but also one hour before services and at six o'clock of the evening before. He also tolled the bell upon notification of the death of a parishioner, at which time the hammer was struck slowly for each year of the deceased person's age.

He also pumped the huge pipe organ's bellows, for without manual action, no church service could begin. Electricity was still a far way off, so lamps and candles provided the illumination in night services. Neither was the organ electrified. Maintaining the proper level on the bellows was a grueling task, especially during the hot days of summer. Needless to say, the work of the sexton played an important part in the church operation and all too often was not appreciated.

The congregation also maintained a separate building on the church grounds. This two-story building provided space for the administration of German Christian education on the first floor and contained a meeting hall upstairs. During the month of June, all school-age children were taught Bible history, Catechism, reading and writing, all in the German language. The pastor at first was the instructor, though in later years he was assisted by others. This training has been of great value to me over the years, though at this time, and especially during extremely hot days, my thoughts often wandered to the old swimming hole. Two events stand out in my recollection of German school days- the fun we had playing monkey tag in the old horse barn and the time I had the wind knocked out of me by a fast ball to my stomach.

St. Paul's old horse barn on Highway 32 and Playbird Road, torn down in the 1930s.

At the close of each summer school, a church picnic was held outdoors. A huge tent was erected and wooden benches arranged in its shade. Recitations, religious songs and some dialogues made up the program, after which a brass band performed. Soda pop, bratwurst, candy and fruit were available throughout the afternoon to celebrate Kinderfest.

It was customary to confirm children by age fourteen. Twice each week attendance at confirmation classes was required with all instruction given by the pastor in German. The Saturday morning class posed few problems, but the Wednesday forenoon session required an excuse from the English day school. Making up the work missed was a source of irritation, but the real difficulty lay in switching back and forth between two languages for two years.

Religious holidays were considered to be extremely important elements of the church year. Easter and Christmas were among those highly regarded events and regularly celebrated, not only for the day, but for two or three consecutive days with church services each day.

For us children, the high point of the year, of course, was the Christmas Eve celebration. Prior to the great day, parts consisting mostly of recitations had been distributed to the children. The church council had spent hours selecting a large balsam tree and decorating it with huge glass ornaments of various colors. Candles secured in holders were attached in strategic places on the extended branches to avoid any possibility of fire. Whenever the huge tree was lit, one of the elders was delegated to be on the lookout for candles that were burning dangerously close to the branches or were expiring.

Great was our excitement on Christmas Eve as the time for the trip to church arrived. In inclement weather, if we used the horses, an extra hour had to be allotted for hitching them to the bobsled. Everyone was bundled from head to toe, for even the ride in the touring car could be downright frigid on Christmas Eve.

Upon arriving at the church, our eyes bugged out at the sight of that huge tree and all of its candles flickering in the chancel of the church. All this glee was slightly dimmed at the thought of having to march up front to deliver lines, since I was not given to facing an audience without trembling knees and wavering voice.

The warmth in our hearts added to the heat from the lamps and scores of candles plus the largest crowd of the year usually sent the church thermometer soaring to its upper limits. All of this added to our discomfort and that of the many babies that made up a large part of the audience. Somehow the two hour Christmas program could never end soon enough for me.

Apprehension changed to bliss when at the conclusion of the service each child received a bag filled with nuts, candy, an orange, an apple and a tablet. The orange was always deeply appreciated since purchased fresh fruit was a rarity in our home. The long ride home was interspersed with comments on the program and conjecturing about the gifts that awaited us under our own tree. All this ended as Mother turned the key to open the door to the parlor where none had dared to venture all week.

Our tree also was decorated with a variety of colored candles which my Father carefully set ablaze by first lighting one candle and then passing the flame to all the others until the entire tree was bedecked with flickering tapers.

While Father kept a watchful eye, checking for branches too close to the candles, Mother would distribute the carefully selected presents, mostly articles of clothing, to us. In some cases a shirt or tie had been borrowed for the program and we were cautiously reminded of the fact. Some toys were among the gifts, but they were few and far between. By the time a few nuts and some candy were enjoyed and Father was extinguishing one candle after another as they burned down to the holders, we got the message that another glorious Christmas Eve had run its course. We were informed that the Christmas Day service was as important as Christmas Eve's service in the celebration of the birth of the Christ child and it was time for bed.

Church Picnics

The rural community at the turn of the last century offered little in the way of entertainment or diversion from the humdrum of everyday life. It was only natural that occasions, such as Kinderfest or Missionfest, at church became an annual high in the lives of the children of the congregations.

Not only was it the wind-up of four weeks of summer school during the hot days of June in the case of the Kinderfest celebration, but it was also a welcome change from summer's endless chores usually associated with the farm. The day before usually meant some preparation since invariably roast chicken was on the noon day menu. Butchering, plucking and cleaning the unlucky birds was a ritual that often required some help from the older children though the parents generally performed the greater share of the chore.

Early on Sunday morning the kitchen stove and oven were fired up for the baking of the chicken as well as one or two homemade pies. Though church services first started at 10 o'clock, this was not a day to oversleep or get a late start in the barn. By the time morning chores and the baking were finished and everyone donned their best Sunday clothes, it was high time to leave for church.

With our contribution to the sumptuous meal still steaming, we all piled into the Model T, carefully hanging on to the dishes that were cradled in clean dish towels for insulation.

As we approached the school where the food was always prepared and served, the big tent suddenly swung into view. It had been erected by the council members during the preceding day and was studded with long wooden benches. Here among the small forest of trees it would provide shade and protection from the elements while the festivities went on.

After quickly disposing of the prepared foods in the schoolhouse basement, the family assembled in the church for the service with its appropriate message by the pastor. On Kinderfest days, the school children usually occupied the balcony from whence they burst forth in songs like "Weil Ich Jesu Schaflein Bin" or "Fang Dein Werk Mit Jesu An" at the appropriate times in the service.

Except for a few farmers who had noon-time errands to attend at home, everyone including guests from neighboring congregations lined up for the noon meal served by the Ladies' Aid. Several settings usually were necessary to accommodate the large crowd. The menu not only included home grown delicacies, but also "store bought" wieners, a real treat for some of us.

After all the tables had been cleared and the last of the dishes were put away, the afternoon service was rung to order. In the case of Missionfest it meant a second service, sometimes in the second language. On Kinderfest day a group of strong men would carry the school organ out to the tent before the start of the program. The afternoon was devoted to songs, recitations and a display of what had been learned during the summer school session under the direction of the hired teacher. A short sermon by the pastor usually was part of the exercise.

At the conclusion of the afternoon church service or the school program presentation, the picnic proper started. Automatically the children forgot the heavy meal of noon time and headed for the concession stands. Here one could buy plums, pears, bananas, candy bars, ice cream and soda for nickels and dimes. Among other goodies, cracker jacks were favorites with their "The More You Eat, The More You Want" slogan and a prize in each and every box.

One of the feature attractions at these celebrations was a concert by a brass band from the Howards Grove church. Stirring religious and march music filled the tent and grounds to the pleasure of young and old who had not yet been exposed to radio, though some enjoyed the luxury of a Victrola at the time.

Children's games were played and awards were given to the winners for their efforts. Adults also could partake of several skill games such as a form of bowling in which the ball was suspended on a rope. Another game featured the art of hurling a baseball at wooden dolls on a mechanical rack.

Long before chore time, the bratwurst fryers busied themselves with their assignment and by and by the families assembled themselves for a final sandwich or two as a fitting end to a memorable day of church festivities and good fellowship.

St. Paul's Church with its square steeple with battlemented tower rail that replaced the original pointed steeple in 1926. This picture is from 1937.

St. Paul's Church, seen at left, rebuilt in 1939 in the original style with pointed steeple.

1950- New Pastor Is Installed Sunday at Millersville

The Reverend O.W. Heier was installed as pastor of St. Paul's Lutheran Church at Millersville Sunday evening, April 9, with ceremonies conducted by visiting clergy.

The Rev. L. Koeniger of Manitowoc delivered the sermon while the installation was conducted by the Rev. E. G. Behm, assisted by the Reverends Hartwig and Koeniger. W.W. Gleschen of Manitowoc served as toastmaster at the banquet held at the school hall at Millersville following the services.

The Rev. Heier is a graduate of Northwestern College at Watertown and graduated from the Lutheran Seminary at Thiensville in 1935. Prior to his coming to Millersville he served as pastor of Our Savior's church at Jamestown, N.D.

Pastor O.W. Heier

1952- Church is Remodeled
Sheboygan Press

The St. Paul's Evangelical Lutheran Church, located one mile south of Millersville on Highway 42-now 32- in Sheboygan County, is currently undergoing a remodeling job which will cost an estimated $30,000. The entire inside of the church has been repainted, new lights and heating system installed, new floors laid and a basement added. New pews, rugs, altar tapestries will be added before the renovation is finished. Two side entrances have been added to the exterior of the church as well as new archways and steps. The basement of the church includes an entirely new kitchen and meeting hall. Previously only part of a basement had been dug and used as a furnace room and coal bin. The present church building was constructed in 1881 making it 72 years old. Before that time the congregation had used an old wooden structure still standing to the south of the remodeled church. The Rev. Otto W. Heier, pastor of the church, said that it would celebrate its 90th anniversary this summer when the work is finished.

1952- Millersville
Sheboygan Press

When St. Paul's Lutheran Church at Millersville observed its 90th anniversary on Sunday, over 1,000 people attended the triple festive services. Student Donald Bitter, Thiensville Seminary, a son of the congregation, was guest speaker in both English and German services held at 9 and 10:30 that morning.

The Rev. Fredrick Thierfelder, pastor of Immanuel Lutheran Church, Black Creek, also a son of the congregation, was guest speaker at the 2 o'clock services. In the evening a sacred concert was held at 8 o'clock for the dedication observances. Bruce R. Backer, principal at Zion Evangelical Lutheran Christian day school, Rhinelander, was the guest organist.

August 1956
Sheboygan Press
Accepts Call to Crete, Ill.; Hold Farewell Party Sunday

Farewell services were held at St. Paul's Church in the English and German languages Sunday morning. The Rev. Mr. Heier has accepted a call to Crete, Ill. where he will serve the congregation of Zion Lutheran Church. The family will leave Millersville the early part of September. The farewell sermon was based on I John 2:24-25. He was installed April 9, 1950 and has served St. Paul's congregation the past six and one-half years. He is a graduate of Northwestern College at Watertown and the Theological Seminary at Thiensville. Prior to his call to Millersville, he served as pastor of Our Savior's Church, Jamestown, N.D. Vacancy pastor will be the Rev. E.G. Behm of Kiel, who also was in that capacity seven years ago, when the late Rev. H.A. Kuether was forced to resign from the ministry because of ill health. Services are scheduled for 8:30am in English and 9:30am Sunday school.

The Rev. and Mrs. O.W. Heier and daughters, Marilyn, Suzanne and Lynda, were feted at a farewell party Sunday evening.

Members of St. Paul's Evangelical Lutheran congregation, Millersville, of which the Rev. Mr. Heier has been pastor for the past six and one half years, gathered in the church parlors for the occasion.

Master of ceremonies, the Rev. E.G. Behm, pastor of Trinity Lutheran Church, Kiel, addressed the group and introduced various speakers. The church choir sang several selections, "Jesus, Savior Pilot Me," "Jesus Lead Thou On" and "God Be With You Till We Meet Again."

Alfred Bitter Sr., secretary of the congregation, briefly addressed the group and others who spoke were the Rev. Elden Bode, pastor of St. John-St. Peter Lutheran Church, Cleveland, who told about the pastor's past life, the Rev. Donald Bitter, a son of St. Paul's congregation, now pastor of Good Shepherd Lutheran Church at Fond du Lac, and Mrs. Ewald Grunwald, president of the Ladies' Aid Society.

Other speakers were the Rev. L.H. Koeniger, pastor of First German Lutheran Church, Manitowoc whose address was followed by brief farewells of Karl Bohlmann and Walter Schneider, by representing the choir members and Miss Allene Kaemmer of the Sunday School staff.

After Mrs. Heier spoke briefly, Louis Perronne, church president, presented gifts to the pastor and his family. The Rev. Mr. Heier then addressed the group with inspiring farewell sentiment, by Dr. Henry Koch, Zion Church. Morrison and senior members of the Synodical conference offered the closing remarks.

Members of the church council and their wives were in charge of the social hour held after the program.

October 1956
Installation services for the Rev. Henry G. Meyer, new pastor of St. Paul's Lutheran Church, Millersville were held on Sunday evening with the pastors E.G. Behm and Donald Bitter officiating. Delivering the sermon and assisting with the installation was the new pastor's aged father, Professor John P. Meyer of the Thiensville Theological Seminary. A reception was held with his wife and daughter, Marie, who came from Elroy, Wisconsin, where he had been serving the Zion Lutheran Congregation. Their son, Henry Meyer is attending the Academy at Mobridge, South Dakota.

New Members of Church Council Are Installed
January 1959
Sheboygan Press

Millersville- Newly elected members of St. Paul's Lutheran Church Council were installed during church services on Sunday morning by the pastor, the Rev. H.G. Meyer.

They are: Roland Schomberg, chairman; Donald Schroeder, secretary; Karl Bohlmann, treasurer; Paul Lindemann, trustee; and Lester Sprenger, board of education.

William Prigge, who for the past 35 years has been janitor and custodian of St. Paul's congregation was honored and surprised when members of the church council ushered him into the front of the church immediately after services on Sunday morning. The congregation presented him and his wife with gifts in appreciation of their faithful services. The pastor gave a short address in which he expressed appreciation of the many tasks and services they gave during the past 35 years. Mr. Prigge, in turn, expressed thanks.

Farewell Party Held For Pastor Of Millersville church and Wife
1962
Sheboygan Press

Millersville- Pastor and Mrs. Henry G. Meyer were surprised at the parlors of St. Paul's Lutheran Church Sunday evening when approximately 135 members of the congregation gathered to honor them with a farewell party. Pastor Meyer who served St. Paul's for the past 5 ½ years accepted a call recently to serve the congregations at Hillrose and Fort Morgan in Colorado. He preached his farewell sermon Sunday morning. Mrs. Meyer was presented with a corsage of white carnations and the pastor a boutonnière.

Henry Meyer
1957 - 1962

Henry Juroff
1962 - 1989

Millersville
1962
Install Pastor Henry Juroff at St. Paul's, Millersville

The Rev. Henry Juroff was installed as pastor of St. Paul's Lutheran Church here Sunday evening. He succeeds the Rev. Henry Meyer who accepted a call to Colorado two months ago. He was installed by the vacancy pastor, the Rev. Gerhardt Cares, of St. John's-St. Peter's Church of Cleveland. Assisting pastors were the Rev. E.G. Behm, Trinity Lutheran Church, Kiel; the Rev. Armin Roeckle, Bethany Lutheran Church, Manitowoc and the Rev. Philip Janke, Bethlehem Lutheran Church, Menomonee Falls, a classmate of Pastor Juroff, who preached the sermon. The Senior Choir sang Speak to me Lord Thy Servant Heareth. About 175 people attended the installation services and reception which followed in the church hall.

St. Paul's Church, Millersville, Will Mark Centennial On Sunday
July 26, 1962 *Sheboygan Press*

MILLERSVILLE – St. Paul's Evangelical Lutheran Congregation of Millersville, whose church is located along Hwy 32, one mile south of Millersville and five miles north of Sheboygan Falls, will observe its centennial Sunday with special services.

The Rev. Otto W. Heier of St. Paul's Lutheran Church at Tomah, a former pastor of the congregation, will be the guest preacher at 8:30 and 10:30 o'clock.

A confirmation reunion service will be held at 2:30 in the afternoon. The Rev. Donald Bitter, St. Lucas Lutheran Church of Kewaskum, a son of the congregation will preach the sermon.

To commemorate this occasion, St. Paul's congregation invited all of its known confirmands whose addresses were available.

New education building at St. Paul Lutheran Church

Millersville Church will Dedicate its Educational Building Sunday- 1967

St. Paul's Evangelical Lutheran Church will dedicate its new $77,779.67 educational building at 3p.m. Sunday.

The Rev. Donald F. Bitter of St. Paul's Lutheran Church of Fort Atkinson, a son of the congregation will deliver the dedication sermon, and the Rev. Henry Juroff, pastor, will serve as liturgist and will make the dedication pronouncement.

The 71 by 63 foot building is attached to the church by a corridor which provides access to the nave as well as the basement. It houses two classrooms, an office, furnace room and rest rooms.

The two classrooms are 28 by 52 and 28 by 28 feet and will accommodate 100 children. Present Sunday School enrollment is 85 with a staff of 11 teachers. The congregation is comprised of 500 members.

Serving on the building committee with Chairman Walter Schneider were Edgar Koeser, Eugene and Robert Kuether and Roland Schomberg.

Edgar A. Stubenrauch and Associates was the architect and Scotty Smith Construction Company was the general contractor. Both are from Sheboygan.

Ground was broken on Ascension Day and the cornerstone was placed in August last year. Several acres of land were purchased east of the church from Theodore Kohl to provide additional parking space and a filter bed for the new building.

Altar view of St. Paul Lutheran Church after the 1973 renovation

View of the rear of St. Paul's Lutheran Church including the balcony.

The Juroffs are Honored for 25th Anniversaries

July 1976

Sheboygan Press

The Rev. Henry Juroff of St. Paul's Evangelical Lutheran Church, near Howards Grove, and his wife were honored Sunday in observance of his 25th year in the ministry and their silver wedding anniversary.

Members of the church council planned a surprise celebration Sunday evening at which the Rev. Gary P. Baumler of Northwestern College, Watertown, preached. The Rev. Philip R. Janke of Manitowoc Lutheran High School was liturgist and music was provided by the congregation's choir and members of the choir at Calvary Lutheran Church, Sheboygan. The group was directed by Theodore Lau, and accompanied by Miss Cheryl Juroff, organist.

After a reception in the church parlors, a group of 240 church members, former classmates and friends gathered in the school and were welcomed by church president Reuben Hoppe. He presented the couple with a monetary gift from the congregation. Pastor Janke was toastmaster for the occasion and introduced special guests.

Pastor Juroff was born at Benton Harbor, Michigan and in 1847 was graduated from North Western College, Watertown. He completed his studies at Wisconsin Lutheran Seminary in 1951 and that same year he married the former Rosemary Martin of Niles, Michigan.

The Juroffs have a son, Timothy Juroff of Waukesha; and three daughters, Rebecca Juroff, a 1976 graduate of Dr. Martin Luther College, New Ulm, Minnesota; Kathryn Juroff, a senior at the same college; and Cheryl Juroff, a senior at Manitowoc Lutheran High School.

Vandalism at
St. Paul Cemetery

A total of 41 tombstones, valued at more than $30,000, were damaged last week in the St. Paul's Lutheran Church cemetery near Highway 32 on Playbird Road, Sheboygan Falls. "This house of peace has been disturbed," said Rev. Henry Juroff, pastor of the church.

It was the third incident of vandalism at the cemetery in the past five years. It was also the most extensive. "The last two times weren't half as bad as this time, said the Rev. Juroff. The incident happened early in the morning of the 4th of July.

The damage wasn't discovered until later in the morning of the 4th by a passing driver. The congregation has been in existence for the past 117 years.

July 3, 1979 Vandals damaged gravestones at St. Paul Lutheran Cemetery, Town Herman.

St. Paul's Evangelical Lutheran Church Will Observe Centennial
Howards Grove
Wednesday, October 3, 1984

Sheboygan Press

St. Paul's Evangelical Lutheran church will observe the centennial anniversary of its church building on Sunday. There will be one service at 10 a.m. The Rev. Donald Bitter of St. Paul Evangelical Church, Fort Atkinson, will be the guest preacher. A son of the congregation, Bitter is president of the West Wisconsin District and second vice president of the Wisconsin Evangelical Lutheran Synod.

The liturgist will be the Rev. Henry Juroff, pastor of St. Paul's since 1962.

Songs by the congregation will include *For Many Years O God of Grace* and *Built On This Rock the Church Will Stand*. The Senior Choir will sing *Great Is Thy Mercy*. The upper grade children will sing *God's Word Is Our Great Heritage* and the lower grades will sing *In Our Church*.

Principal Theodore Berg will direct the choirs and Marjorie Toepel, a daughter of the congregation and Christian Day School teacher at Christ Lutheran Church in Milwaukee, will be the organist.

A fellowship meal will be served at noon. Special invitations have been sent to neighboring sister congregations.

It was in 1884 that the present St. Paul's Church was erected after the first immigrants came to fell the virgin woods and settle in the area.

There is only record of four custodians through all the years, Carl Groth, Henry Kohl, William Rahm and the present William Prigge who with the assistance of his wife is serving his 38th year.

The first organist for the new pipe organ installed in 1884 was Clara Hillemann. Mrs. Milford Henning, the present organist, has served St. Paul's for 28 years and is assisted by Miss Ruth Bitter and Miss Marjorie Toepel.

Christian Neumann was the first sexton and was succeeded only by William Prigge. The present sextons are William Bohlman and Arthur Pieper. Serving on the cemetery board are William Prigge, chairman; Alfred Bitter, secretary; and Herman Knuth, treasurer. The caretakers are Arthur Pieper and William Prigge.

St. Paul's Evangelical Lutheran Church Turns 125
Saturday, August 8, 1987
Sheboygan Press

St. Paul's Evangelical Lutheran Church of Howards Grove on Highway 32 at County Hwy J will celebrate the 125th anniversary of its founding on Sunday, August 16, 1987 at two special services. The 8 a.m. service with the present pastor, the Rev. Henry Juroff serving as liturgist, will feature a son of the congregation, the Rev. Robert Bitter, pastor of St. Luke's Evangelical Lutheran Church of Oakfield. The theme of the sermon will be *Our Heritage of the Gospel's Power*.

A commemoration of Confirmation service will begin at 10:15am with another son of the congregation, Pastor Mark Bitter, dean of students at Northwestern Preparatory School in Watertown, delivering a sermon based on I Corinthians, 1:26-31. Juroff will again serve as liturgist.

Guest organist for both services will be Kevin Loersch, another St. Paul's. The church choir and children's choir, directed by Christian Day School Principal Theodore Berg will provide choral music for both services. Between the two services visitors will have an opportunity to view a display of confirmation pictures dating back to the early 1900s in the Christian Day schoolroom. Visitors can renew old acquaintances as well as view other historical pictures and articles on display.

A 12:30 pm dinner at the Millhome Supper club near Kiel will follow the second service. Former Pastor Henry G. Meyer will offer the table prayer and a short program will feature presentations on the history of the congregation. Robert Simonsmeier, chairman of St. Paul's, will welcome the guests and a roll call of confirmands present will conclude the festivities.

Though the year 1862 is regarded as the official date for the organization of the congregation, some services were held before this date. However, few records exist and thus little is known of the church's history.

Pastor Henry Juroff
By Roland Schomberg

Pastor Henry Juroff served St. Paul's Evangelical Lutheran Church of Howards Grove, Wisconsin from May 20, 1962 until 1989. He was pastor of two congregations in Upper Michigan prior to accepting the call to St. Paul's.

I am 79 years old and have been a life-long member of St. Paul's so I have known Pastor Juroff ever since his arrival in Sheboygan County. I have served in almost every church council position including that of chairman and secretary of the congregation. Living in close proximity to the church, I have also been active in the maintenance of the property and assisting the pastor whenever needed.

In the 27 years of his ministry here, Pastor Juroff took his responsibilities seriously. His sermons left a lasting impression on young and old alike. During his early years with us he made a genuine effort to accommodate the older members of the primarily German congregation who preferred services to be conducted periodically in their native tongue. This practice was discontinued in April, 1976.

Although he made sure his preaching was based on the Word of God and that he followed synod guidelines in his messages to the parishioners, I believe his forte in church matters was his ability to comfort the sick, the dying and the bereaved. His ministering to the homebound and the hospitalized members was to him a very important part of his calling.

Being not only a church member, but also a neighbor, we spent many enjoyable hours together. I am reminded of my family's years in the choir directed by the pastor. After practice sessions he loved to entertain the choir by rendering waltzes and polkas on his accordion for our entertainment.

Pastor Juroff was a mild-mannered man and possessed a good sense of humor. He had a good rapport with children and I am convinced that he left a lasting impression on the youth of the congregation. This was evidenced by his long time promotion for a St. Paul's Christian day school which culminated in the construction of a school building addition to the church in 1967. The one-room school has now grown into a three-teacher facility.

After his retirement, he with his wife moved to Fond du Lac where he continued his calling by administering to the handicapped and ailing in congregations in the area. He has had serious medical problems since he retired, but his strong faith and determination have enabled him to bounce back repeatedly.

Reverend Juroff says farewell, enters retirement
Sheboygan Press,
Saturday, June 3, 1989

The Rev. Henry Juroff will preach his farewell sermon on Sunday. The congregation of St. Paul's Evangelical Lutheran Church, Howards Grove, has shared his leadership the past 27 years. "Now I am retiring from full-time pastoral ministry," he stated, "but no Christian retires from the ministry." Although Juroff was born in Benton Harbor, Michigan he spent most of his childhood with his grandmother on a farm outside Eau Claire, Michigan. "She was influential on my life. I always felt she had the wisdom of Solomon. She never lost her cool, she was even-tempered and always had a solution for the problem," Juroff said. "Then, when I was sixteen or seventeen years old, I was sitting in church one day, listening to the sermon, when I had the desire to do the same thing. After consulting with the pastor … he was delighted. We discussed the length of the school, which is eight or nine years, my heart skipped a beat. But, he assured me it would go fast and it did", he said. "My parents were encouraging and there were no other ministers in our family," he said. After graduating form public high school in Eau Claire, Michigan on May 13, 1942, Juroff entered Northwestern Prep School in Watertown, Wisconsin, graduating in 1947." Then I went to Wisconsin Lutheran Seminary in Mequon. After one year at the seminary, I volunteered to go work a school year in the Apache Indian Mission at Cibicue, Arizona. There I preached and taught school. We were isolated. It was fourteen miles off the highway in a valley of 400 people. I taught grades three to eight. This ministry also included maintaining the school, making certain the kids got a bath once a week. The water was heated by a potbelly stove. It also meant cooking lunch for the thirty-two children. The best thing I can remember about preparing the food was it meant making eight pies and cutting them in fours. Cookies were made by the bushel. It was a good learning experience. It was almost like working in a foreign mission."

After one year in Arizona, Juroff returned to the seminary in Mequon for another year. The next summer he returned to the reservation to assist the resident missionary at White River, Arizona. In September 1950, Juroff returned to the seminary for his final year. He was installed on July 15, 1951 at St. Paul's in Mound City, South Dakota.

"My first congregation in Mound City was 130 members. But I also served four families about fifteen miles away who gathered at a school house on the prairie. I was there for two and a half years." Juroff's next call was to a mission congregation in Battle Creek, Michigan. While there, the congregation built a new church and purchased a house which was remodeled for a parsonage. In April 1958 he accepted a call to a dual parish, St. John's in Florence and St. Paul's in Tipler, Wisconsin.

"We had regular services every Sunday at both churches. Two years later a third congregation was added, Mt. Olive Lutheran church in Iron Mountain, Michigan located seventeen miles from Florence. In those days there was a shortage of pastors and small congregations were banded together." Juroff served the tri-parish until May 1962 when he arrived at St. Paul's in Millersville-Howards Grove. "I feel I have had a full ministry. I am more grateful for it than satisfied."

A new parsonage was built in 1979 at St. Paul Evangelical Lutheran Church, located south of Howards Grove along Highway 32. The home contains 2,400 square feet of living space and includes a pastor's study.

Rev. Jonathan Rossman

The Reverend Jonathan Rossman was installed as pastor of St. Paul's Lutheran Church, Millersville on Sunday, June 25, 1989. Delivering the sermon was the Rev. Ronald Szep of St. Luke's, Little Chute, Wisconsin. The installation was conducted by the Rev. Randal Schoemann, vacancy Pastor. The choir sang *Forever Blest is He*.

Jonathan Rossman was born on June 26, 1956 near Jenera, Ohio, a small town in rural northwestern Ohio. After attending Christian Day School, he was enrolled at Michigan Lutheran Seminary in Saginaw, Michigan where he graduated in 1974. He then attended Northwestern College in Watertown, Wisconsin. He earned his degree there, graduating in 1978.

After working for a year in Jenera, Pastor Rossman began studies at Wisconsin Lutheran Seminary in Mequon, Wisconsin. His year as a vicar was spent at Woodlawn Lutheran Church in West Allis, Wisconsin. During his senior year at Seminary he also served as part-time vicar for St. Jacobi Lutheran Church in the Milwaukee area. May 27, 1983 he graduated from our seminary and on July 10th was ordained and installed as pastor of Salem in rural Sturgeon Bay, Wisconsin.

On August 15, 1981 Pastor exchanged vows of faithfulness with his wife, Linda. Along with three-year old Bethany they look forward to life and work here. They enjoy camping, biking and gardening.

Pastor Jonathan Rossman

St. Paul's of Howards Grove names new pastor
Sheboygan Press
Friday, April 7, 2000

Evangelical Lutheran Church of Howards Grove, March 19. Taves, his wife, Carol and their three daughters recently moved from Janesville, Minn. where he served at St. John Lutheran Church since 1994. A Wisconsin native, Taves served his vicar year in Canada and graduated from Wisconsin Lutheran Seminary in 1989. He then served two churches in Nebraska before moving to Minnesota.

Reverend Kristian Taves

Thursday, April 20, 2000
Sheboygan Press

The congregation of St. Paul's Evangelical Lutheran Church, N7311 State 32 in Howards Grove, welcomed Rev. Kristian L. Taves as its new pastor at a special installation service March 19.

Rev. Taves, his wife, Carol and three daughters, Rebekah, Kathryn and Jackie arrived March 5 from Janesville, Minn. where the 37-year old minister served at St. John's Lutheran Church since 1994.

Born and raised in Wisconsin, Taves served his vicar year in Canada. He graduated from Wisconsin Lutheran Seminary in 1989 and served two churches in Nebraska before moving to Minnesota.

Taves and his family are avid Green Bay Packers fans and together enjoy the hobby of raising and training German Shepherd dogs. They will live in the church parsonage adjacent to the church while focusing on their work at St. Paul's Church and Christian Day School.

Members of St. Paul's and area guests had the opportunity to meet the Taves family at a special reception immediately following the installation service.

St. Paul's 600 member congregation is affiliated with the Wisconsin Evangelical Lutheran Synod.

After 10 years of service, St. Paul's former Pastor Jonathon Rossman accepted a call to serve Christ Lutheran Church at West Salem in January.

Reverend Thomas Unke

The Rev. Thomas Unke became the pastor of St. Paul's Lutheran Church in December of 2005. Pastor Unke was installed on December 11, 2005. Vacancy Pastor Timothy Lindloff of Manitowoc officiated at the installation service. Sermon text was Acts 10:38. "Now We Are All Here." The choirs of St. Paul's sang "Here I Am Lord."

Pastor Unke grew up in Manitowoc, Wisconsin and graduated from Manitowoc Lutheran High School. He also graduated from Northwestern College in 1988 and Wisconsin Lutheran Seminary in 1992.

Pastor Unke began his ministry at Salem Lutheran in Owosso, Michigan. In 1993, he was called to the mission congregation, Beautiful Savior Lutheran in West Des Moines. In 1996 he became the senior pastor at Lutheran Ministries at Tacoma, Washington where he served for almost 10 years, until coming to St. Paul's.

Pastor and his wife, Jackie, were married in 1991 and have been blessed with four children; John and Zach attend Manitowoc Lutheran High School while Emily and Maria attend St. Paul's Lutheran School. Jackie teaches at St. Paul's in the upper grades.

Reverend Thomas Unke

WELS Celebrates 150th Anniversary

Milwaukee- Wisconsin Evangelical Lutheran Synod (WELS) congregations across the United States and Canada will celebrate the synod's 150th anniversary June 11. The celebration, which also observes the 2000th anniversary of Christ's birth, emphasizes going forward in Christ and spans a two-year time period that began in July 1999 and runs through July 2001. June 11, 2000 is the official anniversary Sunday on which members will focus on God's present blessings, and how they can spread the blessing of God's Word to others. Each congregation is observing the anniversary in its own way.

Friday, June 9, 2000

Special Services

St. Paul's Evangelical Lutheran Church, located at the intersection of Playbird road and Highway 32, Howards Grove, will hold special activities Sunday to mark the 150th anniversary of the Wisconsin Evangelical Lutheran Synod and to celebrate Pentecost Sunday.

The church service will be held at 9 a.m. outside under a tent on the church property. Following the service at about 11 a.m., a picnic area will include a roast pig, brats, hamburgers, side dishes and desserts.

There will be games and prizes for children and adults, people dressed in the style of the 1850s era, door prizes, volleyball and plenty of friendly conversation.

St. Paul's is served by the Rev. Kristian Taves.

Roland Schomberg, Ruby Schomberg, Mary Jaeger, Lloyd Jaeger, Lynn Kraemer and Allen Kraemer dressed in costumes of the 1850s.

Church breaks ground on new school, worship site

August, 2002

The Review

"Joyful." This is the word that Carl Toepel, member and former president of the Church Council of St. Paul's Evangelical Lutheran Church of Howards Grove, used to describe his mood and that of his fellow church members. He feels they have two reasons for their elation.

This year the 620 members of St. Paul's are celebrating the 140th anniversary of the organization of their church, a member of the Wisconsin Evangelical Lutheran Synod. And on August 25, the congregation held a ground breaking ceremony for their new 30,000 square-foot church and school complex to be located on a 20.2 acre site at 441 Millersville Avenue, Howards Grove. This property is approximately one-half mile east of State Highway 32 on the south side of the road.

The Bamco firm of Manitowoc is providing architectural services for the project, while Hamann Construction of Manitowoc is the general contractor.

The estimated cost of the project is $2.6 million. "This will be funded by offerings from the heart," said Kristian Taves, pastor of the congregation since 2000.

Al Erickson is project manager of the congregation's building committee, while Don Becker is president. Other members of the committee, organized in May 2002: Al Kraemer, Arno Koeser, Tim Doro, Jeff Schomberg and Ed Radue.

"The new facility will be accessible to all and will offer lots of opportunity for fellowship," Taves said. "The narthex and commons area will be people user-friendly. Our facility may be available for community programs too such as blood drives, voting and youth recreation."

The new one-story, traditional-style facility, more than twice the size of the present building complex, will feature a narthex for the church gathering area; a commons or fellowship hall seating between 75-100 people; a balcony and 65-foot church steeple. The altar area will have a brick façade with a cross that has a built-in halo. The nave, with a seating capacity of 318, will have a sloping floor for better visibility.

The 100-year old art glass windows of the present church building will be removed and placed into the new church facility.

The gym in the facility will serve as an all-purpose room to be used for athletic events, dramas and musicals.

Another advantage to the new building will be additional space for Sunday school classes. "The Sunday school is terribly overcrowded at this time," Taves said. "We are holding some classes in the hallways."

St. Paul's Evangelical Lutheran School presently has an enrollment of 46. The six new school classrooms will be used for elementary-school classes in grades K-8. Confirmation classes, Sunday school classes and adult instruction.

A transition zone between the church and school will include a library and several offices- a general office, administrative office, two pastors' offices and a principal's office. The present school facility does not have a gym or a library.

Toepel is encouraged by the new location of the facility. "It can be hooked up to the village's sewer system," he noted. "And the school is more accessible for students in the Howards Grove area."

With so much to look forward to, enthusiasm is on high. "It's a very special privilege to live at this time to participate in the building of a new church," Toepel said. "Not many people have that opportunity."

Taves agrees, "I think the new facility is a wonderful tool to help us better share the news that Jesus is the Savior. The new facility is much better for sharing God's word. Also it allows for instant growth. We can add on in the future."

The congregation had reason to plan a new facility, since the size and layout of their present church and school were of concern in the church's ability to effectively carry out its mission. Building committee member, Jeff Schomberg, prepared a historical review of St. Paul's current building project.

He noted that the present church was built in 1884 and does not comply with the ADA for entrances, exits, rest rooms and stairs. The size of the worship facility and Sunday school classrooms adequate for the 500 member congregation of the 1950s began to become tight for the 620-member congregation. Also, the building's fellowship hall, which seated about 75 people was inadequate to serve the present congregation.

Thus, in 1993, officials of St. Paul's assigned a Long Range Planning Committee, made up of members of the congregation to explore facility renovations that would improve the church's ability to carry out its mission.

From 1993-98 the committee explored several alternatives. They ranged from renovating the building to make it ADA compliant, to an all-encompassing expansion to meet projected congregational growth. In all cases, the renovation alternatives did not fully meet expectations, and costs were exorbitantly high.

"There were other problems, too. The present church property is landlocked by the highway and has an intersecting street," Taves said.

With those facts in mind, the Long-Range Planning Committee considered exploring the option of a new church and school complex on a new property and in 1999, redirected their efforts toward that aim. "The potential benefits to carrying out St. Paul's mission, and the associated cost, appeared to be of a much higher value, both spiritually and economically, than the renovation alternatives," Schomberg noted in his report.

A preliminary engineering study was completed for a new facility on a property about one mile north of the current church. Then in May 2000 the voters of St. Paul's gave the committee permission to focus solely on a new facility.

With the Long Range Planning committee's work complete, a new Building Committee comprised of members of the congregation, was appointed. The committee's first assignment was to select a property for the new complex.

From July 2000 through May 2001, the Building Committee investigated and explored over 20 sites. The proposed site was to meet certain criteria, such as being located within the Howards Grove community and in a highly-visible location readily accessible and on a minimum of 15 acres. A property was found that met that criteria; The congregation purchased five acres from the Evangelical Free Church of Howards Grove. Marcella Kultgen sold St. Paul's the additional 15.2 acres.

The voters of St. Paul's approved the purchase of the property on May 9, 2001. Closing on the property was completed June 7, 2001.

The voters also approved the necessary funds to perform preliminary engineering work to develop a church design and estimate overall project costs. Construction of the facility is expected to begin in two weeks. Completion of the new facility is slated for spring or early summer 2003.

HG Gets a New House of Worship
Thursday, July 3, 2003 *The Review*

Father's Day seemed an appropriate time for members of St. Paul's Evangelical Lutheran Church, a member of the Wisconsin Evangelical Lutheran Synod, to worship in their newly-constructed church and school facility at 441 Millersville Avenue in Howards Grove.

The new $2.6 million, 30,000 square-foot facility is more than just four times the size of the congregation's former 7,000 square foot church and school building located a tN7311 State 32. That building, which has been sold to a family, was constructed in 1884.

The new building is located on 20 acres of land. This will allow for future expansion, said Rev. Kristian Taves, pastor of the 625 member congregation. We were landlocked at the previous site, which was on 3.2 acres of land. Expansion would have eaten up parking.

The new school, which is three times the size of the former school, has six classrooms for its 50 students in pre-school through eighth grades. The school and church share the same roof, but each facility has its own space. The school includes a gymnasium.

Building Energizes St. Paul's
Tuesday, August 3, 2004
The Tempo

New church and school buildings at St. Paul's Lutheran in Howard Grove were built for the present while remembering the past and being ready for the future. School officials might have gotten a glimpse of that future last school year as approximately 60 students enrolled at the school compared to 45 the previous year- the last in the congregation's old school building.

"It worked out well for us", Principal Theodore Berg said of the new school building, adding that he hopes the trend continues in the years to come. "I don't think it will be as dramatic, but I believe we will continue to grow."

The growth at St. Paul's Lutheran School on Millersville Avenue will continue in the upcoming school year, as the school increases its teaching staff from 3 ½ to 4 full-time teachers. Last year there was a pre-kindergarten/kindergarten teacher, a part-time first and second grade teacher, a third and fourth grade teacher and a fifth through eighth grade teacher. When the first and second grade teacher was not there, those students were grouped with the third and fourth graders.

New Class Configurations

Starting with this school year, the first and second graders will be together full-time and taught by a new teacher, Dorothy Meier. Pre-kindergarteners and kindergarteners will remain together and again will be taught by Jean Porter. Third through fifth graders will be grouped together this year and taught by Luther Curia. Berg will teach this year's sixth through eighth graders. More departmentalization will also take place in science and social studies education for fifth through eighth graders this year.

Teaching The Faith Top Priority

"Religious instruction is a very important part of St. Paul's School. I think a lot of people look at it as a private school, we look at it as a religious school," said Berg. "Everything we do is centered on our belief in Christ. I think we have closer control with the children not only here in school but with their parents."

But school life at St. Paul's Lutheran is not all work. School teams are offered in boys' and girls' basketball and girls' volleyball and school teams also take part in annual soccer and softball tournaments and two spring track meets. The new gym at the school has helped not only those sports but also in scheduling and conducting regular physical education classes.

The gym also helped students stage the musical, "Bach to the Future" this past spring as part of the school's music education. A local piano teacher offers instruction at the school for third grade and up and a Manitowoc Lutheran High School teacher offers instrumental lessons for fifth graders and up. Vocal music is encouraged through a junior choir, and some teachers even sing their instructions to students in younger grades.

Through St. Paul's Church, the Lutheran Girl and Boy Pioneers youth program is offered during the school year, including the Buckaroos for young boys and the Sunbeams for young girls.

Art is integrated into the normal class periods until the third grade when it is taught as a separate subject. Women from the congregation often volunteer their time to come into the school to teach special arts and crafts projects.

Computers are also available for student instruction in the new school.

At left: Jesus statue from old church in narthex seen at left.

At right: The altar in the new church

Below left: Mural moved from old church to new.

Below right: Old light fixture from historic photo.

At left: Display case in the church library,

Another view of the library.

The old 1800s light fixture from above the pulpit, the same fixture today is situated in the library.

St. Paul's Sanctuary

This photo shows four former St. Paul's Pastors taken on new church dedication Sunday, June 19, 2003. They are from left, Henry Juroff 1962-1989, Kristian Taves 2000-2005, Jonathan Rossman 1989-1999, and Seated- Henry Meyer 1956-1962.

Thursday, November 8, 1984

Lutheran Church Hangs Plaque in Rededication

A brief rededication ceremony for a bronze centennial plaque took place at St. Paul's Evangelical Lutheran Church, Howards Grove.

It was received in recognition of its century-old church building, and has been placed to the right of the church's front doors. It bears the inscription: *To the Glory of the Triune God we Rededicate this House of Worship in its Centennial Year.*

St. Paul's Church has also been acknowledged as a county landmark by Sheboygan County Landmarks Ltd.

Located in the entrance to St. Paul's church

Church to Present Living Nativity

Tuesday, November 18, 2003

The Review

After dozens of hour in planning casting, making costumes, and constructing a stable, members of 18 committees totaling over 200 people from St. Paul's Evangelical Lutheran Church, Howards Grove are holding final rehearsals for their upcoming "Living Nativity" presentation.

The public is invited to see and hear a live-15 minute outdoor presentation of the Christmas story complete with animals. The event, which is free of charge, takes place December 5, 6 and 7- every 20 minutes from 6-9pm at St. Paul's Lutheran Church, 441 Millersville Avenue, Howards Grove.

The organizers of this outreach saw a program of a Living Nativity at St. Paul's Lutheran Church, Muskego on a WELS connection video and wanted to bring the program to the Sheboygan County area. So they approached Rev. Kristian Taves, pastor of St. Paul's to request that their congregation do a similar presentation.

After going to Muskego to see the Living Nativity presentation there, the organizers spoke with the coordinator of the event, who has since provided guidance for the Howards Grove congregation in preparing for their upcoming event.

The presentation will be held rain or shine. There are three separate casts made up of children and adults. Baby Jesus will be portrayed by a doll. Pastor Taves and some other members of the congregation narrate the program and the church choirs sing the songs.

Advertising for the event has been an all-out effort. On November 2, members of the advertising committee placed posters in businesses throughout Manitowoc, Sheboygan, Fond du Lac, Ozaukee, Washington and Calumet counties. The authentic event will include a census for members of the audience to sign. The school gym will be decorated in the silhouette of the town of Bethlehem and Roman guards will walk the grounds. Greeters will hand out wooden tokens to members of the audience.

This presentation is important because it lets people know Christ was born, said Maryann Hahn, a member of the Living Nativity organizational committee. This event brings people together in a positive way.

Living Nativity 2003

Living Nativity 2004

December 3, 2004

Living Nativity Presented

St. Paul's Evangelical Lutheran Church, 441 Millersville Avenue, Howards Grove, will host the Living Nativity, a live 15-minute outside presentation of the Christmas story with animals.

The Living Nativity scene will be presented every 20 minutes from 6 to 9 p.m. Friday, December 3, Saturday, December 4, and Sunday, December 5.

Admission is free. Refreshments are available. Signed presentations for the hearing-impaired are available December 4 at 6 and 7 p.m. For more information call 565-3780

A Fond Farewell

June 2, 2006

Plymouth Review

Ted Berg, the principal at St. Paul's Lutheran School in Howards Grove, is met with a hero's welcome on the last day of school, June 2, and his last day as their principal and teacher. Berg will retire after 25 years at the school. He also taught upper grade classes.

As a surprise, the school arranged for a limousine to pick up Berg from his home and drive him to school where the faculty, staff and admiring students waited with signs and words of appreciation.

Goodbye is the hardest word

Monday, June 12, 2006

Sheboygan Press

Retirement ends 45 career of St. Paul's principal

Ted Berg spent 45 years helping students realize their potential. On Sunday afternoon the 66 year old Sheboygan resident was treated with a retirement party by the congregation and teachers of St. Paul's Evangelical Lutheran Church and School at 441 Millersville Avenue in Howards Grove. More than 90 of his former students and many friends gathered to wish him well.

"I really don't know what to say. I appreciate everything that has been done for me for the last 25 years, especially the last week in school." During the last week of school, the principal was treated to a cruise around Howards Grove in a white limo before he arrived at school at 10 a.m. to be greeted by students. He was treated to the limo ride as a retirement gift for his 45 years of dedication as a teacher, 25 of which he spent as principal and teacher at St. Paul's Lutheran.

Berg's wife, Karen, said in all the years he was a teacher and principal, his primary concern was always his students. That's all he ever thought about was his kids. He wanted to make sure they had a spiritual core that they needed. Qualities of faithfulness and dedication are what Pastor Tom Unke said he saw in Berg in the short time he has worked with him. He's here in school when the lights go out and everybody's gone home. That leaves an example for Christian people who know him. As former students and parishioners gathered in the school auditorium to share a meal and memories about Berg, he stood at the door for about 45 minutes greeting each person who walked through the door and even posed for photos.

The old and loved St. Paul's Church on Playbird Road and Highway 32 received a new life when David and Mary Daniels purchased the property and converted the buildings into a spacious home and workshop.

Church Activities

Ladies Aid Marks 50th Event

May 1973

St. Paul's Ladies Aid was organized January 25, 1923 when 20 women of the congregation met with Mrs. Ray Kohl as temporary chairman. They chose the name Frauen Verein des St. Paulus Gemeinde Zu Millersville.

At the end of the first year the group had 34 members. All proceedings were in the German language.

In May of 1973 the Ladies Aid marked its 50th event. Four women received special recognition. The charter members seen at the left front, were Mrs. Albert Oetling, and Mrs. Albert Usadel, back row left, Mrs. Raymond Kohl and Mrs. John Boeldt.

1973 St. Paul's Ladies' Aid-- Row 1: Hertha Schwartz, Edna Bitter, Ella Weiskopf, Selma Schomberg, Hulda Kohl, Lily Boeldt, Sarah Oetling, Amelia Usadel, Lydia Sprenger. Row 2: Eleanora Herzog, Margaret Goedeke, Viola Herzog, Irene Henning, Mildred Fenn, Zerlina Melger, Norma Kaemmer, Gertrude Sprenger, Connie Kuether, Janet Radue, Edna Grunwald, Alma Sprenger, Vernetta Grunwald, Magdalena Schneider, Gertrude Prigge. Row 3: Pastor Henry Juroff, Rosemary Juroff, Viola Mueller, Lorenz Sprenger, Hilda Schneider, Rachel Rabe, Florence Muetzelburg, Ruby Schomberg, Elenora Nordholz, Leona Schomberg, Arline Hoppe, Leona Mueller. Row 4: Olinda Schomberg, Verla Peichl, Lenora Gierach, Roma Toepel, Adela Doro, Rose Sprenger, Germaine Doro, Judy Boeldt, Norma Schneider, Olga Neumann, Benita Bitter.

May 19, 1974 Ladies' Aid *Polynesian Review*

Song "Beauty of Hawaii"

Oh, when I hear the strings of that sweet Aki Kauki.
A ceiling from above, holds me tite all night long.
When the Hilo air makes you stay in the moonlite.
I know the reason why paradise on to song.
I love to dance and sing of the charms of Hawaii
And from a joyfull heart sing Aloha to you,
In every note downtown offers a spell of my Island
For then I know that you'll be in love with them too.

Oh you got to see mama's nue nue muu muu
When she's swinging along the beach at Waikiki
It's the biggest attraction down in Honolulu
because it's loaded with her personality.
Mama's muu muu's like a night gown,
with a bulge that's out of date.
but she struts like Miss Hawaii
at the age of 68. Yes
Oh you got to see mama's nue nue muu muu
its the super duper, drupper of the year.
Oh you gotta see mama's nue nue muu muu
When she's doing the hula hula here and there.
Mama's muu muu's driving all the ladies' ku ku
cause it's the answer to a two way girdles prayer
When your starting on a diet and you'd like to eat along,
simply cover it with muu muu and let nature take its course.
Oh you gotta see mama's nue nue muu muu
It's the gapper, flapper, wrapper of the year.
It's the tuti fruity, cuti of the year.

The Ladies Aid of St. Paul Lutheran Church had "Guest Night" Sunday evening beginning with a ham supper. The committee, Mesdames Ewald and Harold Grunwald, Arwin Herzog, Robert Goedeke, Milford Henning and Reuben Hoppe, portrayed several skits and plays in pantomime. "Thru the Year in Song" portrayed each month of the year with a costume display and song by the assembly. The group also entertained at a "Polynesian Review" in Hawaiian settings and costume. *1974*

1974

1. Tiny Bubbles
2. Mama's Muu Muu
3. Colorful Leis (*show*)
4. Hoonanea-to relax (*rocker*)
5. Beauty of Hawaii
6. Queen Liliuokalani *Irene*
7. Queen Emma *Edna*
8. Colorful hula flowers — *Pom Poms*
9. Small gourd hula dance (little girl)
10. Lovely Hula Hands *Arline*
11. Island dancers (grass skirt) *Edna announces*
12. Thus pounds the Poi *Elnora*
13. Cockeyed Mayer *Vernetta*
14. Name Hawaii
15. Show closes with Aloha...

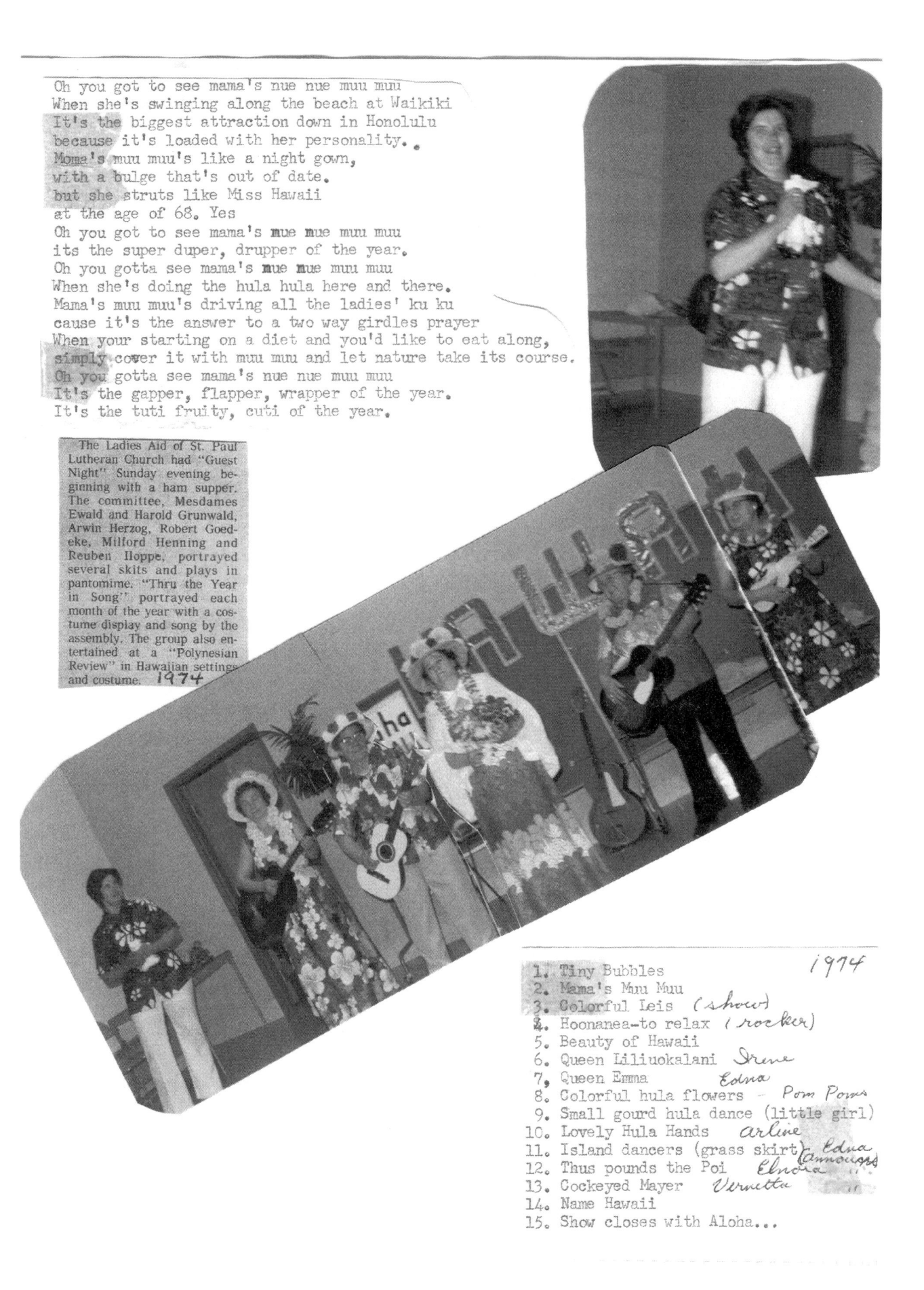

Lutheran Choir of Millersville Honors Members

December 4, 1966

Millersville-Members of St. Paul's Lutheran Church Senior Choir at Millersville, together with their husbands and wives and the Rev. and Mrs. Henry Juroff, honored six members at Johnny's Supper Club Sunday evening in appreciation of their many years of faithful service.

Each honoree was presented with a gift and Roland Schomberg read a poetic tribute he composed. After dinner the group gathered at the parsonage for an evening of songs and games.

Members honored were Mrs. Walter Schneider, Mrs. Otto Schneider, Mrs. Harvey Sprenger, Miss Ruth Bitter, Karl Bohlman and Walter Schneider. All have been with the choir for over 25 years; the first three named have served over 35 years.

Choir Dinner 1966

By Roland Schomberg

It's difficult to find a good excuse
To go out on the town,
Or spend the time in merriment
And to a meal sit down.

For years our choir's been contemplating
An affair such as this,
But somehow it never did materialize
And all plans went amiss.

Then suddenly a completely new idea came forth
When someone did suggest
A dinner that would honor faithful choir members
Who served longer than the rest.

The task began to take monumental proportions
As I was asked to compose
A few lines of verse for the auspicious occasion
And step on no-one's toes.

For there were Norma, Wilma and Gertrude among us
Singing for thirty-five years;
And Walter, Ruth and Carl we remember
For service command our three cheers.

And then there are others who joined in much later
And yet contributed so much.
How can we commend all the older choir members
Without offending such?

Besides all these problems that swept through my brain
One other came to my mind
For our faithful director, the Pastor certainly
I could not leave behind.

So after thinking it over a dozen times or more
I have this firm conviction
That we should probably honor us all, to avoid
Any serious contradiction.

Then I, your spokesman, do now propose a toast
Without a bit of fuss,
To the choir members and Pastor of St. Paul's church
From everyone of us!

St. Paul's Choir- 1930s

Row 1: Adela Doro, Wilma Schneider, Edna Bohlmann, Lydia Sprenger, Elsie Prigge, Emma Bitter.

Row 2: Norma Schneider, ? , Ovila Dengel, Leona Mueller, Eleanor Herzog, Lillie Sprenger, Edna Bitter.

Row 3: Alfred Doro, Arvin Herzog, ?,?, William Prigge, Ernst Sprenger, Henry Schomberg, Harvey Sprenger, Alfred Bitter.

1937 Choir

Top row: Henry Prigge, Harvey Sprenger, Alfred Bitter, Walter Schneider, Norbert Strassburger.

Middle row: Rev. H.A. Kuether, Henry Schomberg, Mrs. Raymond Bitter, Mrs. Alfred Doro, Mrs. Walter Schneider, Mrs. Otto Schneider, William Prigge, William Hehling.

Bottom row: Mrs. Ernst Sprenger, Irene Kuether, Gertrude Boeldt, Rose Boeldt, Doris Kuether, Dorothy Bitter, Edna Hehling, Ruth Kuether, Helen Bohlmann.

1997 Spring Concert wearing new choir robes

Row 1: Bev Gumm, Kathy Bramstedt, Marilyn Eirich, Sara Leu, Katie Hoenecke, Elaine Kuether, Heidi Meyer. Row 2: Rachel Rabe, Karen Berg, Sandy Strauss, Marge Kolberg, Arline Hoppe, Joyce Simonsmeier, Ann Doro. Row 3: Shawn Leu, Gerhard Gierach, Richard Kuether, Reuben Hoppe, Jim Dittmar, Marion Hoard, Eugene Rabe, Marilyn Toepel, Cory Schroeder, Ted Berg.

By Roland Schomberg

Church Centennial - 1984

As I was preparing my presentation, my thoughts kept coming back to one person whose life was interwoven with the chronological events involved in this history. I remembered the tolling of the Saturday evening church bells – one of Bill Prigge's assignments as a janitor of the church for half a century.

I thought of the old basement, mostly unexcavated except for the pipeless furnace areas and the coal pile which Bill utilized to heat the church in time for hundreds of winter services.

I pictured him in the heat of the summer as he dutifully pumped the organ, at first in the fore part of the church and later in the balcony to keep the bellows of the organ at the required level.

As custodian, together with his good wife, he kept the church in immaculate condition though it was but a part of his overall task.

No celebration of this building's centennial would be complete without remembering Mr. and Mrs. Prigge's long, loyal and dedicated service at St. Paul's.

12-5-1940

Despite weather conditions a goodly crowd gathered at the Lutheran school hall to see the three-act play, "Where's Grandma?" given by the Young People's society of the St. Paul's Lutheran church. The cast of characters were: Miss La Verne Herzog as the "Grandma"; Miss Doris Strassburger, the young Jack Worely, the brother, was portrayed by Arthur Strassburger, Jr., and Carol Worely, the sister, by Zerlina Imig; Miss Margaret Bitter took the part of Lucy King, Jack's sweetheart; Miss Doris Kuether, as Arline Truesdale, the girl who wanted to marry Jack; William Prigge, as "Midnight" the colored houseman, and Miss Marcella Neuman, as his wife, the household colored maid and cook, "Dahlia." Between acts a few comical skits with the following people were given: "Morning—trying to get into the bathroom," with Milton Grunewald, Norbert Strassburger, Miss Mildred Nordhof, Richard Kuether, Miss Bonita Heuer and Ernst Pieper; "A Sailor's Technique Skit," with Karl Bohlman and Henry Schomberg, Jr.; and "Passing A Sentence," a skit, with Albert Usadel, Jr., and Elmer Pieper. Musical introduction and intermission was furnished by Miss Dorothy Bitter, Roger Doro and Nyles Perronne. Makeup was by Aaron Mael, and furniture by courtesy of Walter Ahrens. The play was directed by Miss Olivia Strassburger. The play was enjoyed immensely by all who attended both Wednesday and Thursday evenings.

Sheboygan County News

November 30, 1939

The three act play, "An Old Fashioned Mother," given by the Young People's society of the St. Paul's Lutheran church, here at the church school auditorium on Thursday and Friday evenings was largely attended. The cast of characters were as follows: Roma Braun-the mother; Mabel Sprenger- the choir leader; La Verne Herzog- the village gossip; Benita Heuer- the village belle; Doris Strassburger- the widow's daughter; William Prigge- the prodigal son; Henry Schomberg Jr.- the elder brother; Milton Grunewald - a merry heart; Milton Bitter- Enoch; Henry Prigge- county sheriff. The following were the village choir members: Friedola Dengel, Doris Sprenger, Norma Dengel, Jeanette Schneider, Robert Kuether, Elmer Bitter, Richard Kuether, Karl Bohlman and Dorothy Bitter. Selections between acts were offered by Vera Kuether on the piano; violin selections by Arthur Strassburger, Jr. piano accordion selections by Roger Doro and Niles Perronne and vocal and guitar selections by James Doro. Miss Olivia Strassburger coached the play while the Rev. Mr. Kuether directed the singing.

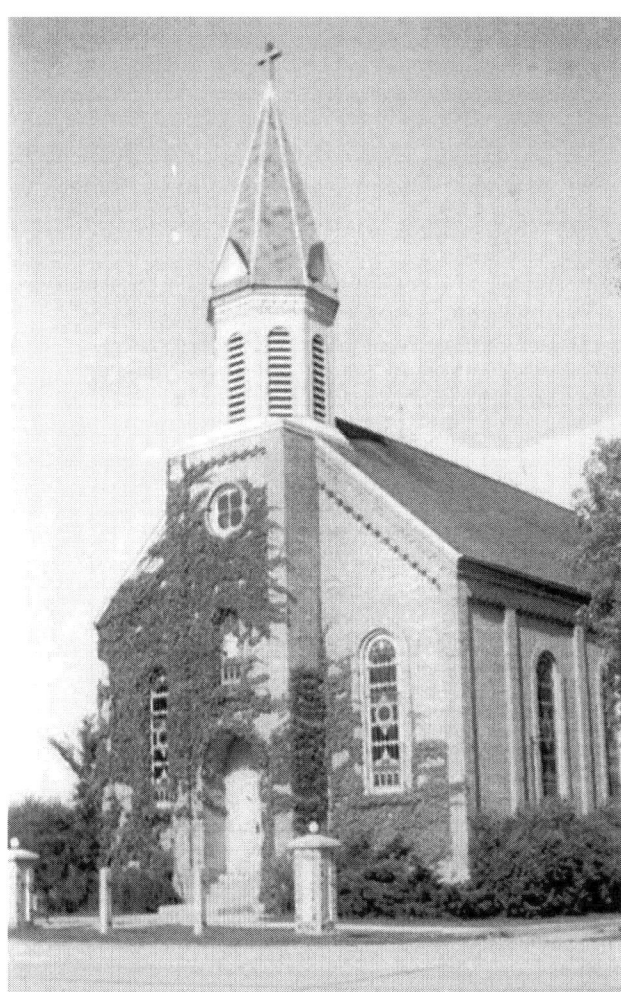

Millersville Box Company

A drawing from the 1875 Sheboygan County Plat book- Henry Mueller's grist and sawmill, section 35, town of Herman.

In 1854, Henry Mueller, the man who founded the Village of Millersville, purchased three and a half acres of land on the bank of the Pigeon River. In 1857 he went into partnership with William Halbach. Here they built the first crude sawmill. This is where the Millersville Box Company is now located.

The mill was destroyed by fire in 1866 and then rebuilt as a cheese box factory. The partnership was dissolved when Halbach moved in 1873.

In 1875 Mueller built a grist mill which he continued to operate with the planing mill until 1886 when he was elected Sheriff of Sheboygan County and moved to Sheboygan. In 1890 he sold it to the Sprenger brothers, Herman and Carl, who soon built a roller flour mill and cheese box factory. The February 6, 1896 edition of the *Plymouth Post* reported, "in spite of the bad sledding and poor conditions of the roads, the farmers in our area have hauled a high pile of tree trunks in front of Mr. Sprenger's mill in Millersville, the pile is so high that one would imagine it could produce enough lumber to board up the whole world."

On August 8, 1898 the *Post* stated "Saw Mill of Herman Sprenger in Millersville will be closed from the 10th to the 30th of September for repairs and renovation, and will again be in operation on October 1." The Millersville correspondent to a Sheboygan newspaper reported on the severe winter snowstorm of February 20, 1898 and related an interesting story:

> The snowstorm brought some excitement into our village. H. Sprenger had a new harness made at Franklin and offered O. Oetling $5.00 to carry it the whole distance in the snowstorm. Mr. Oetling undertook the job and brought the harness Monday evening. The harness weighs 81 lbs. and Oetling is a man 50 years of age. The distance from here to Franklin is about 5 miles.

This is an image of the original H.C. Mueller(Miller) mill at Millersville. The grist mill at right, the saw mill in the rear, and the cheese box factory is at left. Men in the picture include are William H. Sprenger, Albert Sprenger, H.C. Miller in the white shirt with his arms folded, Udo Nagel, William Damrow, Louis Miller, George Best, August and Karl Apt, Fred Usadel, Louis Ohde and Albert Miller.

Millersville Box Employees-Back Row: August Kueter, Herman Sprenger, August Hammelmann, Albert Erbstoeszer and Arno Usadel. Front Row: Fritz Sprenger, Arthur Usadel, Hugo Erbstoeszer, Armand Kueter and Arwin Sprenger.

Herman Sprenger's Mill at Millersville
Arno Usadel in top window
Rudolph Usadel is the teamster

A Chronology of the Early Years of Millersville Box

1854	Henry G. Mueller built the first grist mill and sawmill.
1857	Mueller and Hallwachs (Halbach) built a sawmill.
1866	Fire destroyed the mill. It was rebuilt as a cheese box factory.
1873	Hallwachs left Howards Grove. Mueller built a grist, planning and flour roller mill.
1890	Mueller sold his property to Herman and Carl, Sprenger.
1898	Herman Sprenger injured his leg while sawing.
1907	Sawmill of Herman Sprenger closed from the 10th-30th of September for repairs.
1916	Mrs. Anna Sprenger Pieper sold to her sons, Fred and Arwin Sprenger.
1916	On December 27, the fire destroyed the mill for a second time and rebuilt it.
1917	Millersville Manufacturing Company was officially formed by its Articles of Incorp.
1925	Articles of Incorporation filed for Millersville Box Company

This house stood next to Herman Sprenger's mill in the early 1900s. Pictured are Herman, Anna, Fritz and Arwin Sprenger and members of a Usadel family.

The old Herman Sprenger mill with the Henry Mueller barn in the background. This image was taken in 1916.

Brother Carl Sprenger died in 1909 and Herman continued with the business until his death in March of 1913. His widow, Anna Sprenger Pieper, sold the business to her sons Fritz and Arwin Sprenger in November 1916. On December 27, 1916 the Sprenger's mill was destroyed by fire. A new building was erected in 1917 and the company was named Millersville Manufacturing Company.

Sprenger's Mills at Millersville are Destroyed by Fire

December 27, 1916

Fine Grist and Saw Mill and Cheese Box Factory Burn to the Ground Shortly Before Noon Today --- Cause of Fire a Mystery But May Have Started from a Hot Shaft in the Box Factory --- Calls Sent to Howards Grove and Sheboygan Departments for Assistance --- Loss Will Reach $15,000 With but Little Insurance --- West Wind Saved Little Village from Destruction

Fire of unknown origin destroyed the grist and saw mills and cheese box factory of Herman Sprenger and Sons at Millersville shortly before noon today, causing a loss of $15,000. Very little insurance was carried on the buildings.

The fire was discovered at 10:30 o'clock this morning by Henry Berth, an employee of the firm, who, together with three other men, was working a short distance from the mill. Seeing a cloud of smoke suddenly issue from the building, he summoned the other men and they attempted to rush into the factory, but were driven back by the terrific heat caused by the burning wood. Only two minutes before the smoke was seen, an employee had been in the mill, but he discovered nothing unusual. It is thought the fire was caused by a hot shaft, although this opinion has not been substantiated.

The flames broke out in the cheese box factory, a frame building 75 x 50 feet which was built adjacent to the grist mill. The saw mill and an engine house were built close to the other two structures and quickly were enveloped in flames. The fire spread so rapidly that dozens of men who rushed to the scene were unable to lend any assistance. Nothing could be done and the flames were left to do their worst. The Howards Grove Chemical Company was notified and arrived within half an hour but it could afford no help.

Luckily a strong wind was blowing from the west. The burned buildings were located on the extreme east end of the village. Had the wind been from the east, the entire village would have been wiped out.

…The total destruction of the buildings, added to the loss of over 50 barrels of flour, 500 bushels of rye and wheat and a carload and a half of cheese box lumber, brings the damage to $15,000. The machinery was partially destroyed and heavily damaged. At 12:30 o'clock this afternoon the ruins were still smoldering and the lumber piles were still burning…

In October 1925 the business was sold and the Millersville Box Company articles of incorporation were filed. Arwin became the overall manager in the box manufacturing plant and Fritz became manager of the firm's lumber yard. At this time and in the 1940s farmers could also bring apples to the Box Company to be pressed for cider.

Above: 1910 State of Wisconsin tax bill for Herman Sprenger for a total of $42.46. The taxes covered the grist mill, saw mill and box factory valued at $5000.

Below: Interior view of Sprenger's cheese box factory.

Above: Herman Sprenger's invoice from The Sheboygan Auto and Supply Company and at right a photo of Arwin Sprenger, Fritz Sprenger and Walter Mueller in Sprenger's 1910 Studebaker. This photo was taken in 1913.

Sheboygan Press- December 27, 1916- Fire of an unknown origin destroyed the grist and saw mills and cheese box factory of Herman Sprenger and Sons at Millersville shortly before noon, causing a loss of $15,000. Very little insurance was carried on the building. Photo at left by Arno Usadel.

Millersville Manufacturing after the 1916 fire.

Millersville Box Company yard in the 1940s. From left to right- Henry Mueller's grainery, Fritz and Arwin Sprenger's three-car garage, chicken coop and pig building. Fritz and Arwin Sprenger's houses in background.

Millersville Box Factory Is Razed By Fire Saturday

November 15, 1947

Fire leveled the Millersville Box factory early Saturday evening at the height of a driving snowstorm, causing a loss estimated in excess of $100,000 and leaving 60 employees jobless.

Fed by the stocks of cheese boxes and unfinished lumber inside, the fire quickly swept the 100 by 120-foot two-story frame structure. The countryside for half a mile in all directions was bathed in a lurid, twilight as the falling snow reflected the glow of the fire…

The fire was discovered about 5:10pm by Henry Mueller whose farm buildings stand 100 feet west of the factory. As he stepped outside for a moment, he noticed an odor of smoke in the air and guessing that it came from the box factory he hurriedly summoned the Millersville Fire Department.

By 5:20 smoke was pouring from the building and a few minutes later flames burst through. Fanned by the high wind, the fire had leveled the structure by 6:30pm an 80-foot smokestack rising form the boiler room of the plant had been so eaten away at the base that it toppled and fell across the main blaze.

…At the height of the fire the second floor gave way, and hundreds of the round cheese boxes cascaded down. A gasoline pump at the northwest corner of the building caught fire, and the few gallons of gasoline in the part above the ground burned fiercely.

Officers at this time were Emil Klemme, President; Otto Sprenger, Vice President; Arwin Sprenger, factory manager and Treasurer; and Walter Mueller, Secretary. Preferred Stock was sold at this time.

In 1948 a new factory was built of concrete block replacing the old wooden building, with additions in 1956 and 1970. A new office building was erected in 1950 after being in the front part of the carpenter shop since the fire.

After the 1947 fire the Feed Mill business was sold to Bitter-Neumann. The construction of wooden pallets was added in 1956 and the company discontinued making cheese boxes in June of 1969. On February 15, 1997 at 12:35am fire was discovered again. The east portion of the building was saved, and employees didn't miss a day, helping with the clean-up and continued making pallets.

The plant was completely up and running five months after the fire. After the charred building and two side structures were razed, they were replaced by a new 100 foot by 185 foot structure allowing the company to house all of the manufacturing processes- sawing, assembly, storage and shipping under one roof. A dust collection system was added and an automatic heating system has replaced the old wood burning boiler. A factory office and employee lunchroom were added. In 2005 a heat treating trailer was purchased to comply with regulations for international trade. In addition to heat treating pallets they make, they also offer contract heat treating of pallets, crates, boxes and other wooden packaging containers.

Raging Fire And Snowstorm Combine To Make Unusual Picture

Nov 15, 1947

A raging fire and a raging snowstorm conspired Saturday evening to make the picture above as the cheese-box factory at Millersville burned to the ground. All records in the office at right were lost, together with all the machinery used in making cheese boxes. Cheese-boxes stored on the second floor of the peak-roofed section in the center of the picture fell into the inferno below when the second floor collapsed. Insulation on the power lines leading to the building burned through and gave spectators an electrical display. Buried embers continued to smolder Sunday and broke out in flames again Sunday evening, to bring the Millersville Volunteer Fire department in another hurried call to the scene.—Sheboygan Press photo.

Millersville Box Company before 1947 fire.

Millersville Box before the 1947 fire.

Sheboygan Press

January 13, 1955

When a venerable alderman loses his clothes and runs out into the winter air in his birthday suit, that's news.

It happened to the Dean of Sheboygan's Common Council, William H. Sprenger, but it was some 68 years ago (1887) and Bill was neither an alderman nor venerable, but a mere youth of nineteen years.

The incident, a painful accident, but Bill recalls it now with humor.

He was working at the Millersville mill, which was sawmill, grist mill, and cheese box factory in one. He had gone into the mill to clean out a clogged feed conveyor and made the mistake of stepping too near a spinning shaft. A coupling screw caught his clothes, ripped them from his body and sent Bill flying through air with nothing on but one boot, a torn pant leg and part of one shirt sleeve.

Bruised and bloody, Bill ran to the door of the mill and called to fellow employees in the yard. They helped him into the boarding house. A teamster made a quick trip to Howards Grove for a doctor, and Bill, sore all over, suffered while the Doc poked and prodded in search of broken bones

There were no broken bones, but Bill had a deep cut in the palm of his hand, and the doctor without anesthetics, put 23 stitches in the cut. Bill remembers objecting strenuously not at the pain of the needle but at the long thread the doctor pulled through his flesh at each stitch.

The accident put Bill in bed for weeks. It was 12 days before he could be taken to his home a mile or so away. But even before his hand was healed, he was back on the job at the mill.

Cheese Boxes

Cheese boxes, seldom seen these days, were once a necessary item in the production and transport of cheese. Boxes in the early days were delivered by horse and wagon carrying perhaps 450 boxes on a load. They would travel perhaps 25 miles one way, starting at about 3 a.m. and returning late at night. By 1954 they averaged three loads a day carrying 625 boxes a load and made a 25 mile trip in less than three hours. The factory first employed 10 men who made 500 boxes per day, but by 1954 the payroll had risen to 56, 14 of whom were women, and two to three thousand cheese boxes were produced.

The making of cheese boxes was a very interesting process. In the early years, logs were first put into a vat filled with steaming water and then later a steam vat for 20-24 hours to loosen the bark. The softened logs were cut to the correct lengths necessary for the type of box to be made: Cheddar, Long Horn, Daisy, Midget, Mammoth or Young America. After the bark was peeled and removed from the logs, they were hoisted by a chain hoist and placed into the veneer lathe and centered on the lathe spindles. As the lathe was put into motion, the log would rotate slowly toward the lathe cutting knife, and pieces of veneer, ½ inch thick would come off the log until the log became fully round. These smaller pieces would be used later for staves. The log now being fully round would produce veneer in a continuous piece. A man would operate the veneer lathe, and four other people were involved as the veneer would be cut. One person on each side would take it to the veneer clipper, and the other two would have to be ready to tear or flip the veneer and another long piece of veneer would be started to be taken to the clipper. Here the veneer would be cut to the correct width needed for the type of box to be made. Also some of the smaller pieces of veneer were cut for making the cheese box covers, and strips for the bottom of the box. Others were cut for staves that had to be stapled between two pieces of veneer which would strengthen the box. The veneer would later be put into a machine for a round cheese box. The Albright machine was used to make the complete box.

A cheese box display showing a variety of sizes.

The cheese box and covers had to have wood bottoms made of hard wood. Lumber had to be resawed which cut the boards into ½ inch thickness. Then the boards were put through a planer and sized to 7/16 inch thickness. From there the boards were taken to the cut-off saw where they were cut to the length needed. They were then put through a matcher, which put a tongue and groove on each side of the board. Then the boards had to be pounded together and cut into the size needed for the type of box being made.

A Sprenger Cheese Box label. Note the telephone number- Telephone Rural 7- 1 Short, 1 Long.

As the veneer and wood bottoms were ready, the wooden bottoms were put into the Albright machine, the bottom being clamped between two circular disks. When the disks rotated, a saw cut the squares into a round bottom for the box, then a steel drum came forward over the cut round bottom. The stapled veneer was placed into the drum and the veneer was bent around the drum. After completing its cycle the machine stapled the two ends together. Then the bottom strips were nailed to the bottom of the box by a nailer every 3 to 4 inches.

The making of the cheese box covers was similar to the making of the cheese boxes. The boxes and covers were then placed on a conveyor belt which went to the second floor and to the dry kiln. Before the 1947 fire a large heated room existed on the second floor. In earlier years veneer and boxes were often placed outside to dry in warm weather. Before the automated machines were used, in the earlier years more primitive methods of making cheese boxes were used and nails were used instead of staples.

Millersville Box preferred elm logs for production because elm had all the properties necessary to make a good veneer. The walls of the cheese box were made of a three-ply veneer, and the top and bottom were made of heavy board. The construction was extremely strong as it had to withstand the pressures exerted when a head of cheese weighing between 70 and 78 pounds was shipped.

Photos at left: Employees of Millersville Box Company sawing logs. 1940s. Looking west past the Knoener home seen in the background at left.

Photo below

Millersville Box girls 1942- Top row, left to right- Jeanette Schneider Valenstein Boedeker, Gladys Erbe Zunker, Arline Sprenger Hoppe, and Bernice Sprenger Thomson (standing). Bottom row, left to right- Elaine Herzog Rautmann, Doris Oetling Goetsch, Norma Klokow Grunewald, Lila Mae Toll Herzog and Eunice Schneider Dirks. Bernice worked at Bitter-Neumann in the office.

Millersville Box Company Picnic 1942

Picnics were held on the lawns of Fritz and Arwin Sprenger.

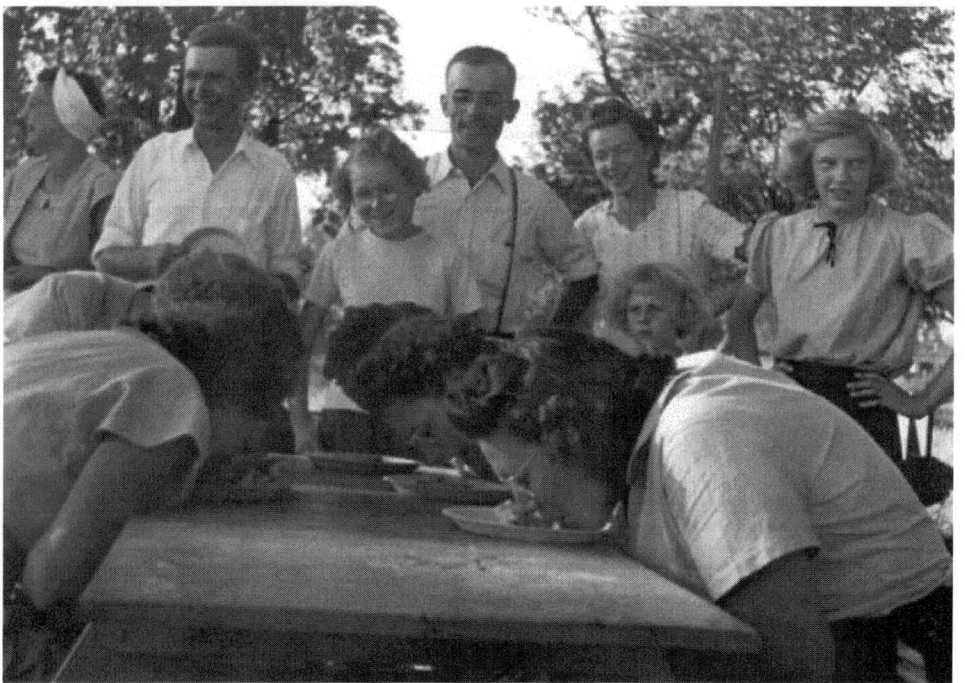

Millersville Box Company Picnic
1943

Migrant workers from Jamaica in 1945. During WWII workers were in short supply in the United States so men were brought in to work at Millersville Box Company.

They stayed in Plymouth during their stay. The girls with the men are Doris Boeldt Edler, Adela Heusterberg Damrow, Doris Oetling Goetsch and Evelyn Heusterberg Sprenger. The little boy is Eugene Sebald.

Millersville Box Employees 1949

Front row: Arwin Sprenger, Bob Tuschl, Caroline Sprenger, George Sprenger, Norman Klein, Herman Berth, Norman Scheibl and Gilbert Klein.

Second row: Martin Grunewald Sr., Carol Mae Klein, Norma Wuestenhagen, Arno Grunewald, Hertha Schorer, Harvey Schorer, Fritz Sprenger, Lester Sprenger, Hulda Berth, Norma Grunewald and Elroy Grunewald.

Third row: ?, Milton Sebald, Irene Sebald, Reuben Hoppe, Walter Klokow and ?

Gathering at the new Millersville Box Company facility after the 1947 fire.

The company entertained cheesemakers and employees after the 1947 fire. Music was by Carl's Trio.

Above: 1954 - Honored for 25 Years- The Millersville Box Company entertained the employees, their husbands and wives at a six o'clock turkey dinner at Kober's Hall, Howards Grove. Gilbert Klein was the honoree who had just completed 25 years of service. He was presented with a gold wrist watch.

Below: From left: Arwin Sprenger, Lester Sprenger, Gilbert Klein, Arno Sprenger, Fritz Sprenger.

Millersville Box Employees, 1950: l to r: Fritz Sprenger, Edgar Boeldt, Elroy Gruenwald, John Ney, Martin Grunewald, Herman Berth, Bob Tuschel, Clarence Illig-on truck- ?, Walter Klokow, Gilbert Klein on top of truck, Next row down, George Sprenger, Milton Sebald, Bottom row, Henry Goedeke, Otto Brendel, Hertha Schorer, Joe Kultgen, Arno "Limpy" Grunewald, Norman Scheibl, Norma Klokow Grunewald, Irene Sprenger Sebald, Norma Klein. Sitting- Carol Mae Klein Bender, Caroline Sprenger Hickmann, Eldora Boeldt Desmith, Marian Schomberg Roethel, Norma Wuestenhagen Wehrmann, Hulda Berth, Bernetta Gorsege Rautmann. Top row standing- Edward Mueller, ?. Marvin Scheibl, ?, Carl Mueller, Lester Seifert, Eldon Kalk, Walter Brendel, Reuben Hoppe, Lester Sprenger on tractor, Arwin Sprenger.

Millersville Box Company in 1954- To the left foreground are the offices and display room. Beyond that is the lumber warehouse and next to that big building is the carpenter shop and saw filing room. To the right center is the box factory where cheese boxes are manufactured and stored. To the far right out of the picture is the new garage.

Sheboygan Press
February 14, 1997
By Pam Hinman

Fire Claims Millersville Box Factory

Firm deciding whether to rebuild after third destruction in long history

Howards Grove- An early morning fire gutted a major portion of the Millersville Box Company in Howards Grove and company officials said they will talk with stockholders before deciding if the plant will be rebuilt.

Firefighters from eight municipalities battled the blaze at the wooden pallet manufacturing company at 931 Millersville Avenue. The fire was first spotted at 12:35 a.m. by a Sheboygan County Sheriff's deputy on routine patrol.

Howards Grove Fire Chief Leonard Schwinn said the company building has an older portion where saws and other equipment are housed and a larger, new portion used as a warehouse for packaging and shipping. He said the older portion of the building was gutted in the blaze.

Millersville Box Company is one of the county's oldest, continually-operating firms with its beginnings traced to Henry Mueller's sawmill in 1854. For years the company made cheese boxes before turning to making wooden pallets for use in shipping and storage.

Dennis Sprenger, plant manager, was unavailable for comment, but foreman Gerry Rietbrock, a company employee for 20 years, said officials will be meeting with stockholders to determine what the next step should be. "We're just going to take it one step at a time", he said. He expects the 20 employees will be able to return to work within a couple of days for stapling pallets together.

This morning's fire was the third in the company's history. The plant was destroyed by fire in both 1916 and 1947. After firefighters arrived on the scene, they concentrated on saving several other buildings, Schwinn said. He credited the fire doors that separate the old portion from the new with saving the warehouse.

Along with the Howards Grove Fire Department, the other departments assisting were Franklin, Ada, Cleveland, Haven, Elkhart Lake, town of Sheboygan Falls and Johnsonville.

The fire was still not extinguished at 7a.m. and Schwinn said firefighters resting at the village's firehouse were going to relieve those still on the scene. Because they have been unable to get inside the building, the cause of the fire has not yet been determined, Schwinn said.

1997 Fire and its Aftermath

February 15, 1997

Sheboygan Press

By Michael Bayer

Howards Grove- …Friday, plant manager Dennis Sprenger said the company would survive again, this time after an early morning fire destroyed a building used to process wood for the pallets.

Just hours after firefighters from eight area communities doused the flames, employees scrambled to ship completed pallets. Late Friday afternoon, the Wisconsin Energy Company restored electricity to company offices. Meanwhile Sprenger and other company officials made plans to resume operations, perhaps as early as next week.

"As soon as we get the OK, we're going to go full speed and rebuild the gutted building," Sprenger said.

Ironically, the two-story structure destroyed in Friday's fire was built after a blaze destroyed the factory in

1947. Then, as now, a Sprenger was in charge. Dennis Sprenger's grandfather, Arvin Sprenger, ran the plant for many years, and his father, Lester, is still president of the publicly held corporation.

… He said many of the company's 23 employees would return to work Tuesday or Wednesday after electricity was restored to the plant. Business manager, Kevin Reinemann said the company would be able to serve customers by purchasing preprocessed lumber and assembling pallets with equipment undamaged by the fire.

The company's insurance adjuster was scheduled to inspect the gutted building today, Sprenger said. An engineer is also expected to look at the damage before the company gets the go-ahead to raze the structure. Sprenger said he hoped to begin demolition Monday or Tuesday. The company would then rebuild on the same site.

A Sheboygan County sheriff's deputy spotted the fire about 12:35 a.m. Friday. Flames quickly spread through the building and hardwood floor that separated the first and second stories…

Howards Grove Fire Chief, Leonard Schwinn said firefighters had the blaze under control about 3 a.m. He also said investigators have not identified the cause or origin of the fire. He also had no damage estimate and he did not suspect foul play.

Millersville Box Company Employees

Upper: Cornelius Will and Melvin Stolzmann in Cut-off.

Left: Hertha Schorer and Dorothy Wiedemeyer in Ripping

Below: Violet Spindler and Leroy Sixel- Stringer Pallet Assembly

The Millersville House
(Sprenger's Tavern - Al Doro's Tavern - Doro's Bar)

Otto Sprenger tending bar.
Bar is located on south wall.

The Millersville House was built by William Damrow in 1876 on the southwest corner of South Wisconsin Drive and Millersville Avenue. Very soon after the structure was completed, Mr. Damrow married Wilhelmina Sprenger and the couple celebrated their wedding in the hall of the Millersville House. The Damrows operated the business for 31 years.

In 1907, their daughter and son-in-law,

Lillie and Otto Sprenger took over the business and the bar became known as Sprenger's Tavern. One of the changes made in the early 1900s was that a tin ceiling was installed in the barroom. In the 1920s the hall was heightened to serve as a basketball court for the community, a basement was added and new maple floor was put in the hall.

In 1937, Alfred and Adela Doro, daughter and son-in-law of the Sprengers took over the business and called it Al Doro's Tavern. The bar was moved to the east wall and a new bar floor was installed. The hall still served as a location for wedding dances, card parties and other various functions.

In 1963, the business passed to a fourth generation when James and Germaine Doro, son and daughter in-law of Alfred and Adela Doro, took over the business. Jim and Germaine modernized the barroom to better accommodate their customers and remodeled the hall which now would also be used for banquets with homestyle cooking. Several major improvements were made to the old summer kitchen including adding a grill and broaster. Tasty sandwiches were served daily in the barroom. The popular place now became known as Doro's Bar. Upon Mr. Doro's death in 1993, Germaine ran the business alone until her retirement in 1995.

Tad and Diane Goedeke purchased the business from Germaine Doro in 1995 and renamed it The Millersville House, which was its original name in 1876. The new couple took out the downstairs living quarters. The kitchen was renovated. A new grill and other modern facilities were installed to accommodate more people. The living room area was turned into a dining room which can seat 30 people. In 2001, Tad and Diane leased the building to Justin Koenig and Brian Picard who ran the business for 2 years.

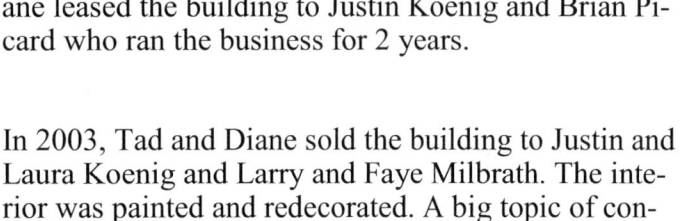

In 2003, Tad and Diane sold the building to Justin and Laura Koenig and Larry and Faye Milbrath. The interior was painted and redecorated. A big topic of conversation to new people, is the old tin ceiling, which was installed by Laura's great-grandfather, Faye's grandfather, Arno Usadel, in the early 1900s. They have become known for their fish fries, broasted chicken, tacos and wings. The original name was kept, which is The Millersville House.

James and Germaine Doro

The Millersville House was once again sold in 2006 to Shawn Baumhardt, who changed the name to Bummy's Haus. The bar remains a place for friendly socializing. The hall still serves as a place for banquets, dances and many family gatherings. The building is one of the few tavern-hall combinations left in the county.

James and Germaine Doro's wedding dance in the hall.

Tending bar: Adela Doro, Frederick Sprenger.

Alfred Doro tending bar.
Bar is located on east wall.

Millersville House

The Millersville House has entertained a lot of people in its 100-year history, and it is one place that can be truly called a labor or love. Its first owner was a carpenter who held his wedding dance in the hall after he built it.

One of the older tavern-hall combinations in Sheboygan County, the structure was built a century ago in 1876 by William Damrow. The two-story building also included living quarters and several upstairs rooms for boarders.

In addition to building his own hall and celebrating his wedding in it, Mr. Damrow was also a musician and was able to provide accordion music for many of the other dances held there. Damrow was born near that portion of Howards Grove then known as Millersville. His wife, the former Wilhelmina Sprenger came over from Germany in 1864 with her parents.

Their daughter and son-in-law, Lillie and Otto Sprenger, took over the business in 1907 and it soon became known as Sprenger's Tavern. The Sprenger's kept the boarding house going, farmed the adjacent land and established a horse breeding and trade business.

For many years, Mr. Sprenger led the Millersville Fireman's picnic parade on his favorite Belgian stallion. Another generation emerged in 1937 as the Sprenger's daughter and son-in-law, Adela and Alfred Doro, assumed control of the operation, and the business passed to a fourth generation in 1963 when James and Germaine Doro took over.

At left: Justin Koenig tending bar

Below: Tending bar: Adela Doro, Frederick Sprenger.

Arno Usadel's Tin Shop

In 1912, Arno Usadel built the first tin shop in Millersville. It was a two-story structure built on the south side of Millersville Avenue between Bitter-Neumann and Doro's Tavern. Upon his death in 1918, a victim of the influenza epidemic, the building was leased to Adolph Kaemmer and then sold to Roland Neumann in 1920.

Left: The Arno Usadel Tin Shop

Top: Interior View of the tin shop with Arno Usadel on left and Hugo Erbstoeszer at right. Behind them are milk cans they manufacture.

Upper Right: Invoice to Hy Dickmann from Arno Usadel Dairy Goods 1918.

Sheboygan Press Article, Wednesday, August 8, 1962 dealing with the demolition of Arno Usadel's old tin shop on Millersville Avenue.

A FAMILIAR SIGHT IN MILLERSVILLE for half a century, the old tin shop, is being razed to provide parking space for the Bitter-Neumann store. The two-story wooden structure was built in 1912 and housed the village's first sheet metal business.

Landmark Being Razed

MILLERSVILLE — A landmark in Millersville, just half a century old, is in the process of being torn down.

It is the old "Tin Shop," a two-story wooden structure located on the south side of the village street on County Trunk JJ between the Bitter, Neumann store and Doro's Tavern. It was built in 1912 for the first sheet-metal works operated by Arno Usadel.

On his death, his cousin, Roland Neumann, took over the business in 1920. With the outstanding growth of business and need for more modern equipment, the sheetmetal department began to include heating, plumbing, milk machinery, etc.

In 1927 Mr. Neumann incorporated his business into the Bitter, Neumann Corp. As the business continued to grow and a larger shop was required, the company purchased and remodeled the old blacksmith shop across the street —from the late Rudolf Schorer— and it became the new plumbing and heating department headquarters. The "tin shop" was then used for storage. In 1960 Fredrick Boedecker, son-in-law of the late Roland Neumann, in partnership with Carl Harms organized the Neumann Plumbing & Heating, Inc., and are the present operators of the former sheet metal, plumbing and heating business.

The old "tin shop" no longer in use and is being torn down to make room for a larger parking area for the Bitter, Neumann & Co.

Rudolf Schorer's Blacksmith Shop

Shown above is the old blacksmith shop of Rudolf Schorer of Millersville. Schorer sold the building and retired from the blacksmith trade in 1952. He began working in the building in 1901 for Charles Reische who is shown shoeing a horse in the picture above. Reische's son is holding the horse which belonged to George Pieper. The picture was taken in 1899. The shop was built in 1876.

Millersville Landmark to be Remodeled

When going through Millersville on Highway JJ you will see in progress the remodeling of the oldtime blacksmith shop owned and operated by Rudolph Schorer one of Millersville's oldest residents. This building has recently been purchased by a sheet-metal heating and plumbing shop, office and showroom which has been operating at Millersville since about 1920.

In tracing the origin of the building we find that the late William J. Kohl built a 20 x 30 foot wagonmaking shop way back in the 1870s. This was situated across the street about where the present sheet metal shop stands. In 1876 Charles Reische built a blacksmith shop 20 x 30 feet right next to it. In 1901 Schorer became employed for Reische as a blacksmith and in 1902 he purchased both the blacksmith shop and the wagon shop.

He moved them across the street and remodeled them into one 50 x 54 foot building where he continued the blacksmith trade. His first employee was Fred Klemme, the retired policeman now living in Omro; then followed Schorer's two brothers, Louis and Fred, Gust. Mog and Paul Wehrmann.

When the wagon and woodwork business became in greater demand he hired Herman Burhop of Howards Grove, who worked for him as a wagon maker and repairman for 13 years. With the coming of tractors and new machinery, business became slack along the woodwork line so Schorer and his son, Harvey, operated the blacksmith shop alone until he retired and sold it in 1952.

Mr. Ferdinand Schneider going shopping at Kohl's store before seeing his girlfriend in 1908.

THE SHEBOYGAN PRESS, Wednesday, August 8, 1962

A FAMILIAR SIGHT IN MILLERSVILLE for half a century, the old tin shop, is being razed to provide parking space for the Bitter-Neumann store. The two-story wooden structure was built in 1912 and housed the village's first sheet metal business.

Landmark Being Razed

MILLERSVILLE — A landmark in Millersville, just half a century old, is in the process of being torn down.

It is the old "Tin Shop," a two-story wooden structure located on the south side of the village street on County Trunk JJ between the Bitter, Neumann store and Doro's Tavern. It was built in 1912 for the first sheet-metal works operated by Arno Usadel.

On his death, his cousin, Roland Neumann, took over the business in 1920. With the outstanding growth of business and need for more modern equipment, the sheetmetal department began to include heating, plumbing, milk machinery, etc.

In 1927 Mr. Neumann incorporated his business into the Bitter, Neumann Corp. As the business continued to grow and a larger shop was required, the company purchased and remodeled the old blacksmith shop across the street —from the late Rudolf Schorer— and it became the new plumbing and heating department headquarters. The "tin shop" was then used for storage. In 1960 Fredrick Boedecker, son-in-law of the late Roland Neumann, in partnership with Carl Harms organized the Neumann Plumbing & Heating, Inc., and are the present operators of the former sheet metal, plumbing and heating business.

The old "tin shop" no longer in use and is being torn down to make room for a larger parking area for the Bitter, Neumann & Co.

Millersville Cheese Factory and Millersville Co-op

In 1886, John Erbstoeszer built a cheese factory and sold it to his son Edward in 1887. Erbstoeszer was proprietor until 1914 when the Millersville Co-op was formed and bought the cheese factory.

Herman Hessler was cheesemaker for Edward Erbstoeszer. Cheesemakers for the Millersville Co-op were Louis Perronne (1915-1918), August Dedlow (1919-1928), Arthur Berth (1928-1934) and Norbert Dassow (1934-1936).

The upper story served as a social center for several years and was known as the Community Hall. Bitter Neumann bought the building in 1942 and closed the alley between the two buildings and enlarged their store.

The cheese factory is the second building in, right next to Bitter-Neumann.

Bitter-Neumann Company

Bitter-Neumann and Company's First Store

July 1954- Millersville- In 1887 when William J. Kohl started his small grocery store in Millersville, he might have had a dream of some day being the biggest and best market in the county. Had he still been living today, he would have seen his dream realized.

In 1922 Mr. Alfred Bitter bought the business and for five years Mr. and Mrs. Bitter worked at doing everything they could to satisfy the wants and desires of the community. It has probably been this unswerving desire to have what the people want in stock at all times that has made the business grow.

The business did grow. By 1927, only five years later, the demand for sheet metal work and plumbing caused Mr. Bitter to join with Mr. Roland Neumann and Walter Mueller to form the present Bitter-Neumann Company. This union has meant a great deal to the outstanding growth of the business and has helped to spread the name throughout the county. Just as the grocery enlarged to include hardware, appliances, yard goods and work clothing, plus toys for the children, the plumbing and sheet metal departments have grown to include such things as milking machines, barn equipment and a wide selection of plumbing fixtures.

Another department had also been expanding as the demand for mixing and grinding of feeds became popular. The old grain warehouse was completely changed over in 1935 and was developed into a grain mill. Modern machinery was moved in and the custom mixing and grinding of the feed as the farmers wanted it was another Bitter-Neumann service. As in the past, fair dealing and prompt service made this business grow despite strong competition. The farmer was quick to realize that he could have this chore done and also accompany the Mrs., while she did the shopping. They could get two things done at one time and would not have to run all over the county to do it.

As more and more people got the Bitter-Neumann habit it became necessary to carry larger stocks and have a greater variety of merchandise. By 1942 the old store was bursting at the seams and there was only one thing that could be done. The store was considerably remodeled and enlarged and the old cheese factory to the east of the store was absorbed and made into a new addition. This new space was utilized for a larger hardware and building materials department and also developed into an appliance showroom. All of the major appliances such as stoves, refrigerators, etc. were lined up for the customers' inspection.

The Bitters Celebrate a Flourishing Partnership

1982 - A partnership formed 60 years ago today by a Millersville couple has resulted in 35 direct descendants and a flourishing business enterprise. Alfred and Edna Schneider Bitter of 1302 Bittersweet Lane were married February 5, 1922, at St. Paul's Lutheran Church in the Town of Herman by the Rev. Louis B. Mielke.

Nineteen days earlier on January 17 Alfred went to town to make the deed for a store and residence that has become well-known throughout the area as Bitter-Neumann and Company. Their four children, Harold and Alfred Jr. (Butch) who run the store, Margaret Zuege of Wisconsin Rapids, and Donald, a minister at Fort Atkinson, will host an open house for the couple from 3 to 5 p.m. Sunday at Doro's Hall.

Attendants who were present are Hilda Schneider of Millersville and Walter Herzog of Brillion. Also present will be their 17 grandchildren and 14 great-grandchildren. Both were born on farms in the Millersville area, he on September 4, 1899, and she on March 24, 1900.

Alfred said he purchased the store and a four-bedroom house, lock, stock and barrel for $15,000 from William Kohl who was 65 and decided to retire. "My predecessor told me, Keep up your credit. Pay your bills on time. He helped me so much. I borrowed part of the money from my mother and Mr. Kohl financed the rest. We paid if off gradually and increased our inventory as we went along. We tried to meet the needs of our customers. We were closed on Sundays, but if someone got unexpected company, they came to the house to ask for a loaf of bread or whatever else they needed. We were glad to oblige", he said.

The Bitters formed a partnership in 1927 with Roland Neumann, who owned a sheet metal shop and Walter Mueller, secretary of Millersville Box Company. "We chummed together and decided to make one business out of our store and the sheet metal shop. Instead of making several separate trips to Sheboygan to pick up supplies, we did it in one trip", he said. The partnership was dissolved in 1960. Both Neumann and Mueller have since died. The sheet metal shop, Neumann Plumbing and Heating Inc. is operated by Fred Boedecker, Neumann's son-in-law.

Alfred recalls there were three telephones in the village shortly after he opened his business, one at the tavern, one at the box company and one at his store. "An ice storm took down the line between here and Sheboygan. It wasn't replaced. A line came out from Sheboygan Falls about a year later."

Prices, obviously, were substantially less in 1922. The Bitters have receipts that show 100 pounds of 8 penny nails cost $3.75; a gallon of gasoline, 23.3 cents; a 50-gallon keg of vinegar, $9.26; bib overalls, $13 a dozen; cook cheese, 15 cents a pound; mens' suits, $29.19; and shoes, $1.35 to $2.75 per pair.

"I cried when he (Alfred) bought our first radio. It cost $400," Mrs. Bitter said. "And it did a lot of crackling." There was no speaker, just earphones, which were passed around to whoever wanted to listen. Later models sported "a big horn." A favorite station was KDKA in Pittsburg, Pennsylvania. The couple's first dining room set, composed of a table, six chairs and a buffet cost $120 in 1923.

Alfred also recalled The Great Depression. "Prices went down. I stocked up on some items when the prices went down. The next time the salesman came the prices were lower yet. Since people must eat, the grocery store was about all that kept the business going up until about 1933, when things started to pick up again. It wasn't the lack of business so much as the government regulations that made things difficult during WWII. Wages and prices were frozen in that period, and there were food stamps and tokens and rationing of shoes and cigarettes to keep track of," he said.

Bitter was joined in business by his son, Harold, in 1942, and by another son, Alfred Jr. in 1953.

He predicted today's recession is going to get worse before it gets better. Bitter said, "People don't realize what it's all about. There's no use worrying. It has to take its course. Times will be good again in the future."

Although he retired from active participation at the store in 1979, he remains chairman of the board and still visits the store daily. "I don't go there to work, but to poke my nose around. I enjoy visiting with the people, but my big trouble these days is putting names with faces," he said.

Alfred remains active in the Howards Grove Advancement Association and the Fire Department. He served as chairman of the board and president of the State Bank of Howards Grove, where he was as director for 46 years. He also was a vice-president of the Millersville Box Company, fire chief, elder and school board member at St. Paul's Lutheran Church.

Edna is a member of the Ladies Aid and was active in the PTA years ago. The couple has traveled extensively, visiting 37 of the United States, Canada, Mexico, Portugal, France, Austria and Greece. They both knit and crochet, but she specializes in knitting afghans. Each grandchild receives an afghan upon graduation from high school. Alfred specializes in latchhook and woodworking.

Edna has also done a genealogy for the family tracing their heritage to the 1600s. A family Coat of Arms graces their living room wall. She also enjoys corresponding with relatives and friends. Just about every evening the couple plays Sheepshead with friends.

Sheboygan Press

May 22, 1942

Opening At Millersville Is Big Event

Millersville- The most interesting event ever celebrated in Millersville was the three-day opening of the newly enlarged and modernized store of the Bitter- Neumann and Company. On Thursday, opening day, Mr. and Mrs. William Kohl and son, Walter, and daughter, Mrs. Friedola Bodenstab, of Sheboygan, came to extend their personal congratulations. The Kohl family first founded and operated what is now the Bitter-Neumann store.

On Thursday evening the Sheboygan Grocers' Association, headed by the "Umph" Band, with John Herman carrying Old Glory, came marching and serenading down the village street to the tune of On Wisconsin into the new store, much to the surprise and delight of everyone. After about an hour of serenading and congratulations, they left with a final *Aloha Oe* and marched up to Al Doro's Rathskeller where a surprise party was given in honor of Bitter-Neumann and Company. About 150 were in attendance.

From Elmer Koppelmann's book, *Howards Grove, Wisconsin-*

The business continued its growth and eventually included seventy-four employees in sales and service positions. Bitter purchased Neumann's interest in the company when Neumann died in 1957. He purchased Mueller's interest when he retired in 1965.

Throughout its history the store was open evenings, primarily to cater to farmers' time schedules. It has never been open on Sundays. In 1988, Harold Bitter, president of the company explained, "I like to have Sundays off and my employees do too. As long as we can make a go of it, we won't be open on Sunday."

The original building was enlarged each time more space was needed until the business literally outgrew its location. In 1971, a new store was opened in Howards Grove at 714 South Wisconsin Drive, just a half mile from the original store. In 1983, Bitter-Neumann and company opened a furniture and appliance store on North 14 Street in Sheboygan. As late at 1988 the flavor of the old time general store was still to be found.

In 1990 Harold Bitter retired, leasing the grocery store in Howards Grove to Piggly Wiggly, and his son-in-law, Ed Radue continued to run the Sheboygan furniture and appliance store.

One of the most unique sales promotions in which the company was involved offered a free pony with the purchase of a refrigerator. Harold Bitter reminisced in a Sheboygan Press article on January 7, 1989: My uncle sold ponies and they weren't going well, so we made a deal with him and offered a free pony with the purchase of a refrigerator.

We sold twenty refrigerators that weekend, which was a lot at that time, and do you know what? We had those ponies in a little corral outside of the store, and those people spent more time picking out their pony than they did their refrigerator.

The image above shows the popularity of the July, 1964 Bitter-Neumann Sale which featured the gimmick- Buy a Kelvinator refrigerator and get a free pony. Twenty refrigerators were sold that weekend.

Sheboygan County News

April 8, 1939

The Bitter, Neumann and Company very pleasantly entertained their employees and their families at the Roland Neumann Rathskellar on Friday evening. The evening was spent at games, cards, socially and songs. Prizes were awarded to Mrs. Milton Dickman, Mrs. William Prigge, Mrs. Adolph Kaemmer, Mr. and Mrs. Carl Harms and Harold Usadel, the floating prize being captured by Adolph Kaemmer. A very good midnight repast was served to the following: Mr. and Mrs. Alfred Bitter and daughter, Miss Margaret, Mr. and Mrs. Roland Neumann and daughter, Miss Marcella, Mr. and Mrs. Walter Mueller, (the Messeurs being employees) and the following employees: Mr. and Mrs. Adolph Kaemmer and daughter Allene Esther, Mr. and Mrs. Arwin Herzog, Mr. and Mrs. Harold Usadel and daughter, JoAnne, Mr. and Mrs. Harvey Sprenger, Mr. and Mrs. Walter Schneider, Mr. and Mrs. Milton Dickman and daughter Grace, Mr. and Mrs. Carl Harms and daughter Carol, Mr. and Mrs. William Prigge, Miss Winona Harms and Willard Bramstedt. The men were all attired in new grey suits with their names and the Bitter-Neumann Company embroidered in Red lettering. Everyone had a most enjoyable time.

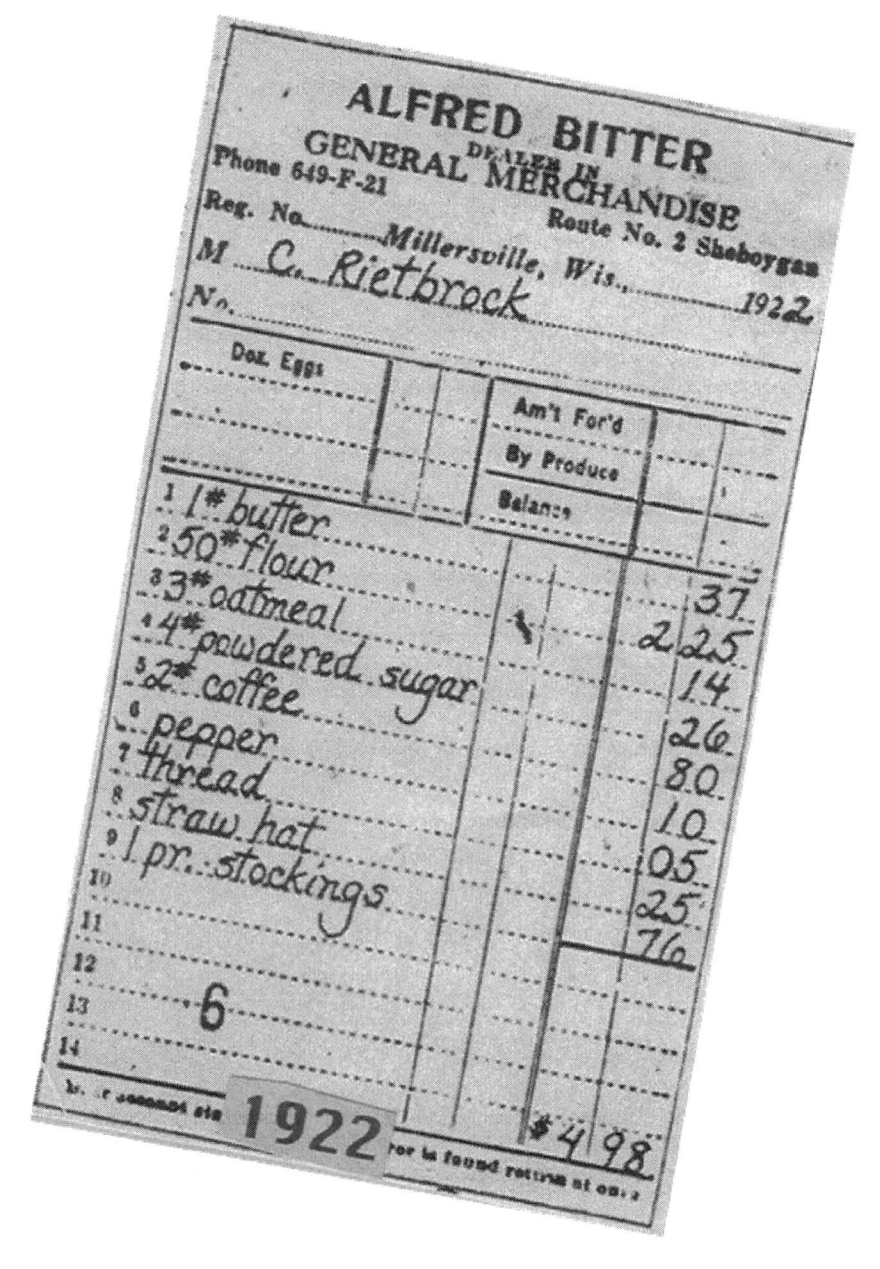

This Week's Bargains at Millersville

CRUSHED PINEAPPLE	7-oz. can 10¢
Schultz Finest DILL PICKLES	½ gallon 49¢
CANE SUGAR	10 lbs. 99¢
HOME MADE BRATWURST	MILLERSVILLE lb. 59¢
8" ELECTRIC FANS	5.95
50-ft. Plastic Garden Hose	3.25
20-ft. Sprinkler Soaker	1.59
Bug Blaster Fly Killer	3 for 1.00
Men's Blue Work Shirts	1.39
Men's Key Overalls	3.69
Boys' Straw Hats 39¢	¼ H.P. G. E. Electric Motors 48.15
100 ft. 16 gauge Heavy Electric Cord 2.98	1 H.P. Master Heavy Duty Motor 79.95
50 ft. 16 gauge Heavy Electric Cord 1.98	36" Lady Baker Divided Top Gas Ranges 99.95

BITTER-NEUMANN & CO.

Your One-Stop Shopping Center

MILLERSVILLE — NO PARKING PROBLEMS HERE

Now is the time to clip your cattle it's easy with an Empire Vac. U. Clipper. We also have a few used clippers, also 1 h. p. gasoline engine for sale cheap.

Bitter, Neuman & Co.
MILLERSVILLE

Mary Heuer and Myrtle Schneider employed at Bitter-Neumann Company having fun in the toy department. 1954

Pig's Tail Alley 1950

Text and pictures below from the book "Howards Grove Wisconsin" by Elmer Koppelmann

On the left is the old Kohl home. Many hours were spent in and around this alley by the children of Millersville.

Pig Tail Alley

Long-time residents of Millersville will recall the term "Pig Tail Alley." It ran between Bitter-Neumann's store and the Mill from Millersville Avenue to South Wisconsin Drive, past what is now Riverside Auto. Riverside Auto is located in Otto Sprenger's barn, which was still in use in the 1940s and 50s and which housed a herd of pigs. They were kept in a fence at the south end of Pig Tail Alley, near South Wisconsin Drive. It was this herd of swine that was responsible for the name of the alley. The alley was used by farmers to load and unload feed at the mill and as a playground for countless youngsters over the years.

Neumann Plumbing and Heating

Upon Arno Usadel's death in 1918, his tin shop was leased to Adolph Kaemmer and in 1920 sold to Roland Neumann. In 1922, Neumann and Alfred Bitter, who owned Bitter's General Merchandise merged and formed Bitter Neumann and Company. As the heating and plumbing business grew, they purchased and remodeled the Rudolf Schorer Blacksmith Shop which was located directly across the street from the merchandise store.

The old tin shop was then used for storage. Neumann Plumbing and Heating, Inc. was formed when Frederick Boedecker and Carl Harms bought the heating and plumbing division. When Mr. Harms retired in 1969, he sold his shares to Kenneth Blindauer. In 1987 Mr. Boedecker retired and sold his shares to Larry Boedecker and David Arnhoelter. When Mr. Blindauer retired in 1994, Boedecker and Arnhoelter bought his shares. Newman Plumbing and Heating is still located in the same place.

2008, Neumann Plumbing and Heating Division.

Tin Shop Crew 1930s

Standing on truck: Arwin Herzog

Standing left to right: Rudolph Usadel, Walter Mueller, Harold Usadel, Harvey Sprenger, Norman Klemme, Adolph Kaemmer, Alfred Bitter, Milton Dickman

Kneeling: Roland Neumann, Carl Harms and Walter Schneider.

Spindler Decorating

Sheboygan Press

Tuesday, January 22, 1991

Spindler's Décor has been in business for twenty-one years, first established at 514 Madison Avenue. Both Norm and Shirley Spindler had experience in the field of interior decorating. Norm was a professional painter working with his father, Norman Sr. Shirley sewed draperies in their home for neighbors and friends,

After 10 years of business at their Madison Avenue location, they moved into the former Bitter-Neumann building on Millersville Avenue. The structure has plenty of history, says Norm. Half of it was the general store, which is a building more than 100 years old and the upper portion was a cheese factory. In 1940 or 1941 they were connected, built together, he says. Our living quarters are above the cheese factory and there are two more apartments rented out.

The Spindlers had lived in a newly built home down the road on Millersville Avenue, but they decided it was handier to live there. For four years they've been living in this apartment.

Spindler's Décor has a strong Howards Grove customer base, and patrons come from every direction around the village. The Spindlers are invited into many homes to consult on interior decorating. The often plan entire home decorating schemes. They deal in flooring, wall covering and window treatments. Shirley acts as sales clerk, decorating consultant and drapery seamstress, while Norm works part-time on the road, installing window treatments or supervising flooring installation,

The window treatment portion of Spindler's business is unique, says Shirley. We sew our own draperies here. Everyone advertises that they have their own workrooms, but those aren't in the stores, they're at the manufacturers. We actually do our own sewing.

The advantages are that we have positive control over workmanship. And the waiting period is shorter. We can make alterations or adjustments the same day. That time factor is important. The Spindlers' daughter, Joy Baumann, works part-time in the sewing workroom at the store. Their other two children, Fay and Gene, live in Two Rivers and Seymour, respectively.

…The busiest months of the year are October through December and the spring months. Norm says it's easy to tell when someone is hosting confirmation or graduation parties or Christmas parties, because that's the most likely time for them to look into home decorating changes.

The Spindler's sold their business to Doug and Kristi Luecke in 2000 after thirty years in decorating service to Howards Grove.

Inside Out Designs, LLC

Local residents, Kristi and Doug Luecke purchased Spindler's Décor from Norm and Shirley Spindler on April 15, 2000. Norm and Shirley retired after being in business for 30 years.

After renovating the interior and updating some displays, the grand opening was held in September of 2000. In 2005, the exterior of the building was redone.

Kristi operates the business along with a full-time designer and seamstress, Gail Butzen. They offer a full line of flooring adding Mannington and ceramic tile, custom designed soft treatment blinds, wall coverings, and custom paints by Pratt and Lambert. They also offer full design service – including personal design and color consultation, space planning and personal shopping.

After three years in business, the store was renamed Inside Out Designs, LLC and incorporates Doug Luecke's business – Luecke Roofing and Siding LLC. There is a sample showroom of vinyl siding, vinyl clad replacement windows and Owens Corning asphalt shingles. Customers can come into the store and check out samples.

The store is open Monday to Wednesday from 9 a.m. to 6 p.m., Thursday from 9 a.m. to 8 p.m. and Saturday mornings from 9 a.m. to noon. Customers may also set up personal appointments at their convenience.

Du Wayne's Auto Body

In 1946 a garage was built by Victor Meyer on South Wisconsin Drive. It was sold to Archie De Becker around 1952. Paul Lindemann bought the garage in 1958 and ran a jeep dealership which was then known as Millersville Motors. In 1965 Lindemann sold the business to Larry and Janice McGray who specialized in antique automobile restoration. He renamed it McGray's Auto Body and used the shell of a 1926 Model T Ford which was mounted on a pole as a business sign. McGray added a steel building to the back of the shop in 1960.

Du Wayne Thiel, who had been employed by the body shop for seven years, purchased the body shop from Larry McGray on March 31, 1973. A remodeling project consisted of adding a new roof and siding done by Du Wayne in the early 1980s. The old concession stand from Riverside Park was moved up to the body shop to increase storage for the business. The business was now known by Du Wayne's Auto Body.

Du Wayne operated the business until his death in 1990. In 1991 the business was purchased by Kevin Prom and continued under the name of Du Wayne's Auto Body for several years. After this, Built-Rite Cabinetry occupied the building until they moved to the former Bitter-Neumann property that had been occupied by Palms Power Center. The Du Wayne's Auto Body property is now a duplex owned by Randy Grunewald and also occupied by Boeldt's Electric.

Built-Rite Cabinetry

Built-Rite Cabinetry, Incorporated has been a constant in the Howards Grove community for the past eight years. Owner and operator, Donald Hersey, started the carpentry shop, which now sits next to the Howards Grove Piggly Wiggly.

Hersey and his staff specialize in custom cabinets, however, they also can make many other beautiful woodworking items for any room of the house or office. With their slogan, "It's your cabinetry, have it Built-Rite" you are sure to receive quality woodwork and services.

Seen here is the old Palm's Power Center, owned by Reinie Palm, once located on South Wisconsin Drive. Palm took over the former Bitter-Neumann Garden Center in May of 1993. The business was a division of Sheboygan Auto Supply, which services small engines, air compressors, starters and alternators. It now houses Built-Rite Cabinetry.

Millersville Feed Mill

From Elmer Koppelmann's Howards Grove, Wisconsin

Milton Wiedmeyer recalled: The feed mill was built by Millersville Manufacturing Company. Later they gave up the feed mill; they didn't want to bother with it anymore, after grinding feed for years for farmers. That's why the taverns had good business because farmers would stop for a drink when they waited for their feed. Alfred Bitter took over the mill business. He combined all his businesses into one enterprise; anything to help his customers.

When Bitter owned the feed mill, Arwin Herzog worked in it. In the basement of the mill, Bitter sold Simplicity lawn equipment. Now the old mill is used by a cabinet maker and as storage for Riverside Auto.

The feed mill was then sold to Badger Hatchery.

Badger Hatchery

From Elmer Koppelmann's *Howards Grove, Wisconsin*

Badger Hatchery was started by the Theune family on North 15th Street in Sheboygan in 1930. It began as a chicken hatchery that later sold feed. Over time the feed business continued to grow and the chickens were all but forgotten except for the name. The company incorporated in 1940. When Wallace Grube and Stan Buyze, a grandson of the Theune's, purchased the mill as a partnership in 1963 they moved the business to Millersville. They purchased the Bitter-Neumann Feed Mill, located on Millersville Avenue in the silver building which is now storage space for Riverside Automotive.

The partners used the old mill for six months while the present mill, located at 1412 South Wisconsin Drive was built in what then was a cornfield between 1963 and 1964. The partnership between Grube and Buyze dissolved in 1968 with Grube becoming the sole owner

Services in 1992 included bulk and bag delivery of feed, grain banking and exchange, and a full time feeding consultant for forage testing and inhouse computer ration balancing.

> September 20, 1963
>
> Excavation has begun here on the new mill that will be erected by the Badger Hatchery, which, since August 15, has been operating the feed and seed department of the Bitter Neumann Company. It will be erected just south of the village intersection.

Millersville Garage

The Millersville Garage, Henry Berth, proprietor, is located at the main crossroads in the village of Millersville. The garage is a new, modern, building containing a repair shop fully equipped with the latest appliances, a sumptuous display and comfortable offices. The garage is operated under the name of Chevrolet Sales and Service Station and Mr. Berth being an enterprising man, has proved to be a profitable and growing establishment in the village. Patrons of this garage are assured of receiving prompt and efficient service. The first garage in Millersville was The Millersville Garage built in 1924 by Henry Berth.

Millersville Garage and Otto's Barbershop

In 1929, Otto Schneider rented the show room of Millersville Garage, located on the northeast corner of Highway 32 and Millersville Avenue, for his new barber shop. In 1936, he purchased the building and continued his barber shop and operating the garage. Frank Holden was the mechanic and others employed there were Al Janke and Russell Boeldt. For a short time in the late 1930s, part of the show room was rented to a dentist. The garage was then leased to Elmer Schmidt from 1947-50. LeRoy Valenstein bought the building in about 1950 for his distributing business. Howards Grove Improvement Company purchased the building in 1967. In 1988, the state bought the building and demolished it in 1994 to widen the highway and install curb and gutter.

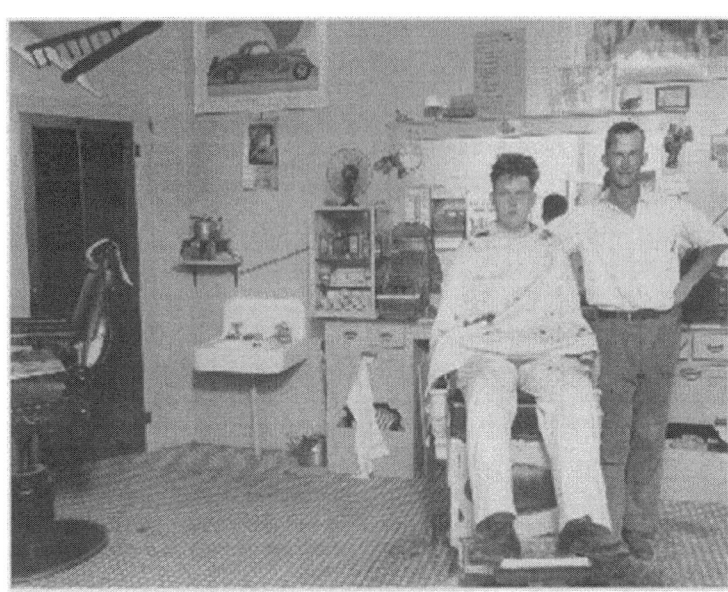

New Car Sales in 1941
Frederick Bartzen ….. $915
John Boeldt……………… $865
Wilbert Dengel ………..$935
Willard Fasse …………..$898
Albert Schneider …… $806
Arno Sprenger …………$865
Paul Wickesburg …… $938
Milton Wiedemeyer…..$914
Herbert Wunsch ……….$853

What'll you have, a haircut, shave, or a tankful of gas? Well, meet Otto Schneider, he can fill your order and a whole lot more. Otto has a barber shop, filling station and garage at Millersville. For the past 15 years he has been barbering and since 1936 he has also operated a garage and filling station in the village. Mr. Schneider has the Chevrolet agency, sells used tractors and cars, repairs all makes of tractors and cars and features Cities Service products.

Howards Grove Improvement Company, Inc.

The company was formed in 1958 by Wayne Goedeke and Lloyd Luecke. It

s location was in the side room of Kober's Tavern on Wisconsin Avenue in Howards Grove. On March 27, 1967, the owners purchased the building previously owned by LeRoy and Janette Valenstein who operated a beer distributorship there. Before them it was owned by Otto Schneider, a barber, and the original owner was Henry Berth.

From 1967 to 1973 the business was run by these officers:

Wayne Goedeke, president

Lloyd Luecke, vice president

Judy Luecke, treasurer

Mary Ann Goedeke, secretary

Wayne and Lloyd were in charge of sales and applications and Mary and Judy were in charge of bookkeeping.

In 1973, Lloyd and Judy left the company. Wayne and Mary continued to run the business there until May 11, 1988 when the state of Wisconsin bought the building because of plans to improve the intersection. The business then moved to 1706 Playbird Road and County Trk Y. In later years, upon Wayne's retirement, the Howards Grove Improvement Company was purchased by Robert W. Goedeke and Tad Goedeke.

The Goedeke sons (Todd, Tad, Robert and Jon) were all employees from the time they were teenagers.

Northeast corner of Millersville Avenue and Highway 32

Looking west across Hwy. 32 towards the old Oetling barn, which was located on the Carl Herzog property.

Ken's Distributing

It was in 1948 when Leroy Valenstein saw an ad in the *Sheboygan Press* offering for sale a beer distributing route. It was Fox Head 400 and owned by Ken Althen- hence the name Ken's Distributing Company.

That same year he picked up Dad's Old Fashioned Root Beer dealership for Sheboygan County. He rented warehouse space on North Avenue in Sheboygan at the Sheffler Trucking Warehouse. One year later he added the Miller High Life Beer Distributorship for Sheboygan and Manitowoc Counties.

When the Sheboygan warehouse was no longer big enough, he bought the Otto Schneider Garage and Barbershop building. Mr. Schneider continued giving haircuts and this meant free haircuts for a while.

During this time, Heileman's Old Style and Heileman's Special Export Beer was added. Then somehow he was talked into being a Graf's soda dealer. The 50/50 soda was a big seller.

Ken's was the biggest wholesaler in Wisconsin for some time. RC Cola and Diet Rite Cola were also added. Again, bigger floor space was needed so LeRoy bought the Otto Sprenger barn. Milford Henning did the remodeling. Six doors were added along with floor space for the trucks.

Somehow word was out that Ken's Distributing had many trucks, employees and warehouse space so more types of beer were added. They included: Jung's of Random Lake, Rahr's from Green Bay, Carling's Red Cap and Carling's Black Label from Chicago and Braumeister from Milwaukee. Expansion continued until Le Roy decided to go into the real estate business in 1972. The trucks, the franchises, and all other related things were bought by Jack Lewis from Cleveland, Wisconsin. Many of the employees went along and worked for Mr. Lewis. The Sprenger barn warehouse was sold to Jerry Simon who turned it into a car repair business.

Employees who worked for Ken's are listed below.

Jerry Bender	Howie Hensel	Wayne Schorer	Ervin Bender Jr	June Platz
Gary Semph	Steve Bender	Vern Koepen	Thomas Usadel	Hans Boeldt
Dave Kraemer	Ervin Valenstein	Karl Bohlmann	Jim Laack	Randy Voland
Donald Damrow	Vernon Reichert	Dave Wehrmann	Wayne Drier	Ed Weigand
Allen Reseburg	Harry Witthuhn	Al Frederickson	Earl Roethel	John Rejolic
Robert Gutschow	Ken Zimmermann	Robert Hansen	Margaret Reische	Joe Zagozen
Jeanette Valenstein				

Bill's Piggly Wiggly

Bill and Mary Schleh of New Holstein purchased the Piggly Wiggly from Harold Bitter of Bitter-Neumann and Company in September of 1990. Bill Schleh's family had been involved in the grocery business since his father, Roman, opened Schleh's Piggly Wiggly in New Holstein. It was here that Bill worked since he was in the eighth grade, starting out as a stock boy. After high school he became produce manager for four years, then frozen meat manager, two years as assistant meat manager, then two years back in produce, and two more as store manager. Mary was the bookkeeper. His two brothers took over operation of the New Holstein store.

When arriving at Howards Grove the Schlehs shared the building with Bitter-Neumann appliance center and hardware store which still occupied half of the building. The Schlehs purchased the business on October 8, 1990, closed the old store and planned the Grand Opening of their new business for three days later.

The Sheboygan Clinic-Howards Grove

First Sheboygan Clinic-Howards Grove

The Sheboygan Clinic, a division of Aurora Medical Group, purchased two acres from Bitter-Neumann for construction of a satellite clinic located just north of the Spargling Clean Car Wash on South Wisconsin Drive and held an open house in November of 1994. In December 2003 the clinic was moved to a new site in Reedsville. A new clinic, built just south of the former clinic, opened in November 2003.

New Sheboygan Clinic Howards Grove

Feldmann Sales and Service

In 1948 Palmer Feldmann started doing custom wood sawing for people, the same year that he married Ruby Bardon. Palmer had a large two-man chain saw that he took from farm to farm to cut firewood. In 1950 the couple bought a farm in the town of Sheboygan Falls and Palmer began selling Lombard chain saws. He also serviced what he sold. Palmer's shop was located in an old summer kitchen heated by an old pot belly stove. During the 1960s Palmer worked periodically at Feldmann Engineering, but he continued to sell saws and other equipment at night.

In 1963 the Feldmann's added Polaris snowmobiles. The whole idea of snowmobiles was so new that for the first two years they didn't sell one new machine. But they used and enjoyed them with their own family. In 1965 they sold five machines and in 1967 thirteen. By 1970 they sold a total of 129 new machines and 75 used sleds.

The business continued to prosper, but on January 8, 1985 a devastating fire wiped out the entire business. Loss was estimated at $500,000. The Feldmann's relocated to Howards Grove at that time, buying a building which had been home to Schmidt's Lawn and Garden at 1014 South Wisconsin Drive. The business was operated by son, Gordon Feldmann and his wife, Doris.

The land itself has an interesting past. Schmidt's purchased the land from the Woepse Orchard. But, Victor Thierfelder from Milwaukee was an earlier owner, purchasing seven acres from Martin and Rosa Boeldt in the early 1940s. He planted 710 apple trees and built a home. His father, William, and mother came to Millersville from Milwaukee before Victor, and they, too, built a home on what is now part of the Howards Grove Fire Department property. Their house was moved to West Bell Avenue. William also planted apple trees and sold garden plants.

Wallo's Auto Service

All in a Day's Work

The Review

Tuesday, November 28, 1995

Located at 804 South Wisconsin Drive is Wallo's, an independent full-service gas station, auto repair shop, wrecker service and used car lot. Wallo's garage has six stalls where repairs are made to vehicle engines, brakes, tires, emissions, etc. He also runs a 24-hour wrecker and towing service. He sells about 50 cars yearly from his used car lot.

In 1979 Skip Wallo bought the business from Orville Schneider- then known as Schneider's Auto Service. Today, Wallo has three full-time employees, but has hired many high school kids to work part-time.

Spargling Clean Car Wash

Two pickups occupy the car wash on Wisconsin Drive.

Varish Chiropractic Clinics

Located on South Wisconsin Drive, the Varish chiropractic clinic held groundbreaking ceremonies in February 2000 and opened in mid-summer of that year. Massage and physical therapy services are also available.

Cleveland State Bank- Howards Grove

Groundbreaking ceremonies launched the construction of the Cleveland State Bank in Howards Grove in September 2005, just north of the Varish Chiropractic Clinic. Temporary banking facilities were located in the former village hall until the new bank was completed in 2006.

Irene Heimann Beauty Shop

Sheboygan Press

April 1, 1954

Make Plans for Open House at New Beauty Shop

Millersville- On April 1 a new beauty shop will open for business at Millersville. There will be an open house from 7 to 10 p.m. A cordial invitation is extended to the public. Refreshments will be served.

Millersville's new beauty shop will be operated by Miss Irene Heimann, who will specialize in permanent waving, hair cutting and styling and will give a complete line of beauty services. Miss Heimann is a graduate of Badger Academy of Beauty Culture in Milwaukee. She is an experienced operator and has been a licensed manager in Milwaukee and West Allis during the past 15 years. Business hours will be from 9am to 6pm on Wednesday, Thursday and Saturday and from 9am to 9pm on Tuesdays and Fridays.

Miss Heimann is a daughter of Mrs. and Mrs. John Heimann, Route 3 Plymouth. The Heimanns, residents of town Herman for the past 30 years, are in the process of completing the first story of their new residence at Millersville. The basement, which is the beauty shop, will be complete by the end of March. The upstairs has been completed for some time and is occupied by Mr. and Mrs. Neuenfeld.

Rita's Doorway to Beauty

Rita Bender, owner of Rita's Doorway to Beauty hair salon, notes that her customers are more like family members. They're not just business customers. The business located at 1020 Millersville Avenue has been in business more than twenty years. (It followed the Irene Heimann business).

Raised on a farm in Johnsonville, Rita's parents are Henry and the late Ruth Rautmann. Following her graduation from Plymouth High School, Bender went to Beauty School in Green Bay. Afterwards she worked as a beauty operator at Schones Haus in Sheboygan for two years; went for her manager's license; and then managed the Schones Haus salon for the next four years.

In September 1974 Bender opened her own three-station beauty shop with one other operator, Katy Dunton. Remembering back, Bender said, "The first day I opened for business I did Mrs. Schaap's hair and I still do her hair today. She comes every week and sometimes I even scold her for driving over if the weather is bad. Her husband brought her for many years and just sat outside and waited until she was finished."

Bender laughingly admits she knows everything about her customers, their husbands and families. "I'm the first one to hear when something is wrong. They know me well, too."

Although Bender and her customers exchange tidbits about their families, I tell the girls to stay away from gossip. The girls are beauticians employed by Bender; Sherry Horness, 15 years; Darlene Meyers, 13 years; Lynn Bogenschild who was hired April of last year. Dunton worked at Rita's for seven years and another operator, Carol Schuette worked at Rita's from 1976-1991. She had some other part-time operators, too.

Looking back, Bender noted, "About 10 customers have been coming the full twenty years. Theresa Rabe and Mrs. Witt are two who have had continuous standing appointments." No matter where she goes, Bender sees people that were customers. "Moms and their little ones come up to me and ask if I remember cutting their hair when they were little girls. I'm doing grandchildren already and am almost going on the next generation." Twenty years ago, people had a standing appointment to come in once a week. Now Bender said it's more like every two or three months. People are more on the go and don't take time for themselves. She said that people do more color now for shine and conditioning- before it was just to cover the gray hair. Today it's healthy looking hair. Permanent waves are given about once every six months and cost almost twice as much as they did twenty years ago. More conditioners are added to perms.

The beauticians at Rita's do haircuts, shampoos and sets. Years ago when the roller set was popular, people couldn't do their own hair at home as easily as now that styles are more casual. Just wash, blow dry and use the curling iron.

Customers at Rita's are of all age groups, children through adults. Twenty years ago, men never came into the shop. Today half of Bender's customers are men. Rita looks forward to people coming into her shop. She's really attached to some of them. When they're sick, she worries about them. If they're late she wonders whether they had an accident. An example of Bender's closeness to her customers is demonstrated when she wants to go on vacation and asks her regulars that if they have anything special planned during that time, she'll change her plans.

As a member of the Cosmetology Association, Bender and her three employees attend all the meetings. They also go to workshops in Green Bay and Milwaukee to preview new cuts and styles.

This is the time of year when school starts and kids begin wearing hats that Rita and the other operators watch for nits and head lice. "I don't know why, but it's always the fall of the year."

Rita's Doorway to Beauty is closed Mondays. Regular hours are 9:00 a.m. to 7:30 p.m. Tuesday through Friday and on Saturday, from 8:00 a.m. to 2 p.m.

A fun day for Bender at her shop is doing a wedding party. "Everyone is having their hair done, including the mother, grandmother and there is so much excitement. It makes me feel good knowing I make someone feel better by doing their hair. My shop has a real family atmosphere, and I like it that way."

Riverside Auto

The building that is now Riverside Auto at 1429 south Wisconsin Drive was constructed as a barn in the late 1800s and owned by Wilhelm and Wilhelmina Damrow. The barn was on the same parcel of land as the tavern, now The Millersville House. In 1907, Otto and Lily Sprenger purchased the barn and tavern.

The barn was sold separate from the tavern in 1937. Otto's son Frederick and his wife Lorena Sprenger purchased it for their pigs, cows and horses. Otto and Frederick were breeders of Belgian horses and Otto was an expert horseman. For years he would lead the annual firemen's picnic parade mounted astride his favorite Belgian stallion carrying an oversized American flag.

The building was purchased by Leroy Valenstein in the mid 1950s and used as a warehouse for the soda and beer distributorship known as Ken's Distributing. Leroy made changes to the building. One remodeling project was in the hay barn. One third of the floor was constructed into living quarters. For many years Bernice Zimmermann lived there.

Leroy's other major renovation was the addition to the building of six overhead doors for storage of his delivery trucks. These were also the loading dock for the soda and beer delivery trucks. These overhead doors made the place ideal for the next set of owners, Jerry Simon and Allen Dirks.

In August of 1975, the building underwent yet another transformation. Jerry Simon and Allen Dirks rented the building from Leroy to start Riverside Automotive. The business started as a six bay repair facility. The size of the building was conducive to business growth. They soon added an automotive parts store that carried name brand and fast moving car and truck parts. Riverside quickly became a full service center for light truck, foreign and domestic automobiles.

In 1978 Jerry and his wife, Rose Simon, purchased the building from Leroy. At this time the partner changed.

Vollbrecht Sheet Metal

After completing the Sheet Metal Apprentice Program through Lakeshore Technical College and Fox Valley Technical College, Mark Vollbrecht worked for area contractors until 1994. It was always his goal to set up his own business and be able to offer the highest of quality in product and service.

Mark and his wife Sandra had moved to the Howards Grove area in 1991. This area seemed like a natural fit for their young family, with schools, shops and churches nearby. The friendly neighborhood atmosphere was one draw to this quaint village. And, when opportunity knocked, Mark and Sandy made the plunge to move to Howards Grove after finding out the Millersville Fire Department building was for sale. The type of building, as well as the close proximity, sealed the deal. Vollbrecht Sheet Metal was in the early makings.

Mark continued to work for area contractors until 1994. At that time, and after careful planning and purchasing of the necessary equipment, Vollbrecht Sheet Metal opened its doors later that year. While the quality of work and service remains the same, Mark has continued to upgrade his equipment and building.

Hennings Restaurant

Milford Henning built a restaurant on South Wisconsin Drive in 1950. The Grand Opening was held in April 1951. Hamburgers and brats sold for $0.25 and steak sandwiches for $0.30. Dinners and plate lunches were served daily. Family-style meals were available upon request. The restaurant was in operation for 1 ½ years. After the business closed the building was leased to Ballhorn Funeral Home for five years. When the lease expired, the building was converted into three apartments.

Gust E. Wiedemeyer
Carpenter Contractor

Gustav Wiedemeyer was a carpenter-contractor. He built many of the houses and other buildings in the village of Millersville. He built houses, hip-roof barns and did general carpentry.

When he moved from Sheboygan to Millersville in 1915 he built his carpenter shop east of the corner of Millersville Avenue and Hwy. 32.

At one point, when Gust was thinking of moving from Millersville to Howards Grove to build a house, Millersville businessmen, Otto Sprenger, Alfred Bitter and Roland Neuman, asked him to reconsider. They worked with him to find temporary housing until his new house could be built.

The temporary housing was offered by Mr. Sprenger. Gust partitioned off the dance hall at Sprenger's Tavern and used the storage area for his kitchen.

Eventually, the shop was rebuilt and living quarters were added. His son, Milton, joined him in partnership in 1933.

When young men of the village wanted to play basketball like the guys in Howards Grove they found Mr. Sprenger's hall was not high enough. They asked Mr. Sprenger if he would raise the roof. They asked Gust to supervise the job. Gust agreed and in order to complete the job he borrowed some blocks and jack-screws. Gathering a labor crew made up of members of the basketball team and men of the village, he spaced the jacks around the roof. Then on his signal each person gave a turn of the screw and in that way was able to raise the roof enough to play basketball. Mr. Sprenger was kind enough to pay for the materials used to secure the raised roof.

Gust retired in 1955 after a long career.

At left is Wiedemeyer's carpenter shop, now remodeled into a house. Its address is 1323 South Wisconsin Drive. At center is Gust's house, 1302 Millersville Avenue, now owned by Diane and Tad Goedeke.

THE WHOLE FAMILY HELPS when the harvest time comes. The Elmer Pieper family, R.1, Sheboygan, gets everyone in on the job. Mr. and Mrs. Pieper (left and foreground) are shocking oats with the help of their 73 year-old uncle, Art Pieper, R.1, Sheboygan, while their son, Richard, 16, operates the tractor and another uncle, William Bohlmann, 74, R.1, Sheboygan Falls, runs the binder. The Elmer Piepers, who live on the west side of Highway 32 just north of Millersville, rent this field from Art. They expect to have 25 ½ acres of oats by the weekend. Commented the elder Pieper, "The oats isn't too good but it could be worse." – (Sheboygan Press photo. 1963)

Clubs

Sheboygan County News

August 30, 1934

The Millersville 4-H club won fourth place on their booth at the county fair. It rated high in quality inasmuch as the club took first prizes on all three articles in fifth year sewing; second prize on thrift project; one second prize, three third prizes and two fourth prizes on second year clothing; a first, a second and a third prize on home furnishing articles and a first and a second prize on patch articles. The girls who exhibited at the county fair are: Pearl Horneck, Lucile Kohl, Esther Sommer, Frieda Sommer and Alice Sommer. Miss Gertrude Prigge is the leader. The club is in existence since 1931, this being their fourth year.

Sheboygan County News

May 2, 1935

The sportsmen of this vicinity gathered at the community hall here Monday evening for the purpose of organizing a club known as the Millersville Rod and Gun club. Officers were elected as follows: William Hering, president; John Markwardt, vice-president; Walter Mueller, secretary-treasurer; Emil Klemme and Herman Kimme, directors, and Adolph Kaemmer, steward. The next meeting is scheduled for Monday, May 13, at the Community Hall and all sportsmen from the surrounding territory are cordially invited to attend.

Walter Mueller shot an eagle having a six-foot wing spread here in the neighboring field Tuesday morning.

Sheboygan County News

January 30, 1936

The Millersville Homemakers met on Thursday afternoon at the home of Mrs. Adolph Kaemmer. The topic for study was on *Color in Dress* with Mrs. Alfred Doro, leader, in charge. Important facts as the balance of color, effect of light on color, effect of texture and color were studied and the choice of becoming colors as suited to the individual skin, hair and eyes was studied with the various shades and samples of materials brought by the leader. Due to extreme cold weather and traffic conditions only a few ladies were in attendance and no business was transacted.

Sheboygan County News

April 19, 1937

Millersville

Mrs. A.E. Kaemmer

The Millersville Rod and Gun club held its yearly meeting at the community hall here on Monday evening. Election of officers took place and the following were elected: Emil Klemme, president; John Markwardt, vice-president; Herbert Thiel, secretary-treasurer; and Herman Kimme and Walter Mueller, directors. There was a general discussion in regard to the digging of wild gooseberry bushes by the P.W.A. workers as being a disadvantage to the preserving of wild life. A week ago the club received and planted five dozen rabbits they had purchased from Kansas. On Tuesday evening the club sponsored a five-reel moving picture at Otto Sprenger's hall, shown by W.T. Calhoun, conservation warden of Madison. Mr. Calhoun also gave an interesting talk on the preserving of wild life and cooperation among sportsmen.

Sheboygan County News
March 1945

The Millersville Junior 4-H girls, Mrs. Clarence Illig, Mrs. Harvey Harms and daughters and Mrs. Adolph Kaemmer attended the second annual Talent Night program at Plymouth High School on Firday evening. The girls presented a Mock Wedding in which Allene Kaemmer acted as preacher, Norma Wuestenhagen as the bride, Margaret Illig as the groom, Gladys Harms as matron of honor, and Helen Schomberg as best man with Jeanette Illig as pianist for the accompanying music.

Sheboygan County News
1945

The Millersville Juniors 4-H club, which was organized on July 24, with Miss Leona Kilborn present at the home of Allene Kaemmer, Millersville had its first meeting on August 21 at the home of the junior leader, Miss Harriet Sprenger, Millersville. Those elected to office follow: Jane Herzog, president; Dorothy Thierfelder, vice-president; Jeanette Illig, secretary; Marion Schomberg, treasurer; Allene Kaemmer, club reporter; Myrtle Schneider, song leader; and Helen Schomberg, cheer leader.

Enrollment cards, projects and record books were passed out by the leaders, Miss Frieda Sommer. Enrollments of projects follow: Miss Harriet Sprenger, junior leadership; food, nutrition and clothing, Jane Herzog, Allene Kaemmer, Margaret Illig, and Dorothy Theirfelder in the first two while Marion and Helen Schomberg, Jeanette Illig, Gladys Harms, Caroline Sprenger, Carol Mae M. Klein, Myrtle Schneider, Shirley Herzog and Mary Heuer are in the clothing group. The next meeting, the last Monday in September, will be held at the home of Gladys M. Harms.

The Millersville Juniors 4-H club held its October meeting at the home of Shirley and Barbara Gabrielse on Monday evening. Annual election of officers took place and officers are as follows: Allene Kaemmer, president; Gladys Harms, vice-president; Carol Harms, secretary; Helen Schomberg, treasurer; and Patricia Sprenger, club reporter; Helen Schomberg and Susan Sprenger enrolled as Junior leaders. A card of acknowledgement was received for the CARE package the club sent recently to Germany. Plans for the hostess card party to be held October 17 were made.

The Review
Thursday, November 14, 1974

30 Years- The Millersville Juniors 4-H club observed its 30th anniversary, Monday, November 4, 1974. Shown from left are Karen Koeser, 4-H Queen; Mrs. Herbert Klemme, Project leader; Mrs. Edgar Koeser, leader; Frieda Sommer, leader.

Millersville Jrs. Observe 30th Anniversary

The Millersville Jrs. 4-H Club girls observed their 30th anniversary with a parent's night at Doro's hall, in connection with their November meeting.

After a short business meeting a distribution of fair prize checks; achievement pins and certificate awards were made by their leader, Frieda Sommer and their 4-H Queen Karen Koeser.

There was a display of project articles made during the year; record books and pictures of the club members kept through the years. A style show portrayed garments made by the girls.

Karen Koeser, president of the club, presented Miss Sommer with a corsage and gifts, one being a 4-H trophy inscribed, "Frieda Sommer, 30 years leader" and another 4-H Emblem plaque inscribed "30 years leader- Millersville Jrs. 4-H club. Mrs. Herbert Klemme, knitting project leader was named for 10 years of outstanding service.

A guest of the occasion was Mrs. Adolph Kaemmer, who had been instrumental in organizing the club 30 years ago. Mrs. Kaemmer addressed the group, recalling a few historic events of 4-H activity in yesteryear as compared with the present. She was leader of the Millersville Rainbow 4-H girls organized in 1931.

Entertainment consisted of a colored slide lecture by Walter Kuester on their recent tour in Holland.

When the girls served a repast to the group, the specialty was a large square cake beautifully decorated in green and white 4-H motif made by Mrs. Herbert Klemme. It bore the inscription "Congratulations Millersville Jrs. on 30th anniversary of your 4-H Club and to Frieda Sommer for her 30th year of leadership.

The Millersville 4-H girls' history dates back to January, 1931 when the very first club was organized and named Millersville Rainbow 4-H Club. It had an enrollment of some 23 girls. Mrs. Adolph Kaemmer was its leader with Mrs. Philip Horneck as her assistant.

The first officers were Ruth Bohlman, president; Pearl Horneck, vice president; Verona Goedecke, secretary; Alice Goedecke, treasurer; Orlita Burhop, cheerleader and Norma Dengel, reporter. Projects then were Clothing I, II and III; thrift, home furnishing and junior leadership.

The club was always a 100% achievement club and partook in all county 4-H activities. They exhibited and had a booth at the county fair in which they won first prizes and many individual prizes; partook in dress revues at county and state fairs; took part in drama; radio programs over WHBL, attended 4-H camp at Camp Rokilio and took part in the fireman parades and 4-H achievement programs. After the Junior Leaders took over and girls became over 4-H age, no club existed for several years.

The present Millersville Jrs. 4-H club was organized in the summer of 1944. Miss Frieda Sommer, an outstanding member of the former club was contacted and became its leader. At that time a foods project had been added, and through the past 30 years the following projects have been carried: Clothing I, II, and Iii with Mrs. Jerry Loersch and Mrs. Charles Teege as helping leaders; Knitting I, II, III, IV and V with Mrs. Herbert Klemme and Mrs. James Burke; leather craft, Mrs. Edgar Koeser; home furnishings, I and III, Mrs. Arno Koeser; food nutrition I, II, III, IV and V, Mrs. Joyce Mattsson; fruit preservation, Mrs. Martin Grunewald; crocheting, Mrs. James Burke; art, gardening and house plants; Mrs. Arno Koeser, Photography II and Junior leadership. In junior leadership Karen Koeser is leader and clothing and gardening while Ruth Grunewald is junior leader in foods and gardening.

During the past span of 30 years the club has been a 100% achievement and honor club for a number of years. Miss Sommer was honored as leader several times and just recently received her ruby pin at the 1974 leaders' banquet at the YMCA.

1974

Plymouth Review
Millersville 4-H

Original Members of the Millersville Juniors 4-H Club pictured in 1944 include, top row: Jeannette Illig, Harriet Sprenger, Mary Heuer, Marian Schomberg, Helen Schomberg and Miss Frieda Sommer, leader; second row: Jane Herzog, Gladys Harms, Myrtle Schneider, Allene Kaemmer and Carol Mae Klein; kneeling: Shirley Herzog, Margaret Illig and Caroline Sprenger.

Miss Sommer was assistant superintendant of the 4-H clothing department at the county fair since 1962. Several girls have been delegates at the 4-H Club Congress at Madison, including Carol Harms in 1955; Debbie DoBas in 1971 and Karen Koeser and Carol Mattsson in 1973. Charlotte Wunsch was selected for Citizenship Short Course at Washington, D.C. in 1965 and chosen home economics girl of Sheboygan County in 1966; Molly Harms was in dress revue at the state fair in 1967; five girls were on the queen's court in 1972 and Karen Koeser was chosen 4-H Queen of Sheboygan County in 1974 at the older youth award banquet.

The club was presented with a 1974 community leaders award at the leaders' award banquet. Besides their various projects, the girls participate with a booth and exhibits and dress revue at the county fair; have a yearly window display for the National 4-H club week at the Bitter Neumann Company store; participate in the music and drama festival in which they took a blue ribbon, and were televised in the music at the fine arts theater program at the University of Wisconsin. They have also sponsored a paper drive in the community for many years.

Graduates of 4-H throughout the 30 years were Judy Harms, who was a member for 11 years; Martha Dobbertin, Joann Rautmann, Joan Schomberg, June Platz and Charlotte Wunsch.

At the first annual meeting of the club in 1946, Allene Kaemmer was elected president and Norma Wuestenhagen was elected vice president. Other officers elected were Helen Schomberg, secretary; Margaret Illig, treasurer; Jeanette Illig, cheerleader; and Carol Mae Klein, song leader. The program at the first annual meeting included a demonstration on how to gather on a sewing machine and a discussion of the topic 'getting rid of insects and pests". The club also discussed their window display and practiced a song they were to sing on the achievement program.

Present officers of the club are Karen Koeser, president; Jodi Beck, vice president; Doreen Jaeger, secretary; Ruth Grunewald, treasurer; Emily Mattsson, reporter and Maria Laack, assistant reporter. Members of the club besides the officers are Kim Boeldt, Colleen Burke, Barbara Entringer, Glenda Feldmann, Donna Grunewald, Loreen Jaeger, Donna, Lisa and Wanda Kumbalek, Maria Laack, Cheryl and Lori Loersch, Carolyn Melger, Debbie, Jill and Sandy Prange.

The club looks back in pride to its accomplishments and in gratitude to their faithful leader, Miss Sommer. Their yearly reports, record books, and reporter's book of activities are a credit to the community.

'Neighbor Club' Marks 25th Event at Millersville

August 18, 1965

Millersville- Members of the Neighborhood Club at Millersville are observing their 25th anniversary this year. It was organized by the late Mrs. John Henning and Mrs. Fred Sprenger in 1940 and their first gathering was held at the former's home.

Of the thirteen charter members, seven are still with the club. Mrs. Rudolph Schorer, retired, Mrs. Ted Schneider, resigned, Mrs. Anna Pieper, Mrs. Henry Mueller Sr., Mrs. Henning Sprenger and Mrs. Fred Sprenger are diseased.

The seven remaining charter members are Miss Elsa Kruse, Mrs. Arwin Sprenger, Mrs. Henry Mueller, Mrs. Walter Mueller, Mrs. Milton Sebald, mrs. Arno Sprenger and Mrs. Adolph Kaemmer.

The group consists of eleven at the present time and those besides the remaining seven are Mrs. Minnie Sheibl, Mrs. Irmgard Sprenger, Mrs. Roy Fenn and Mrs. Arnold Dedering. The group observed the occasion on Wednesday evening with a banquet dinner and party held at Boeldt's Place at Rhine Center with their husbands as guests. Hostesses for the event were the Mrs. Henry and Walter Mueller. Miss Elsa Kruse, oldest of their group was presented with a corsage.

The Neighborhood Club

The Neighborhood Club was a group of Millersville ladies who played cards twice each month, alternating homes. It started in the 1940s and ceased to exist in the 1970s. The following was written in 1971 about the group.

Our Neighborhood Club

I wonder if you ladies know
That it's over thirty-one years ago,
That this our Neighborhood Club was started
And to this day, has not yet parted.

Twas Frieda and Anna Sprenger who
First thought of being hostess to
A club, at which we all could play
A game of cards to pass the day.

Twere thirteen ladies who started out,
Every other Thursday it came about.
Each summer a picnic lunch was spread
At either Sprengers or Muellers homestead.

As years went by, we then observed
An annual banquet, and were served!
A committee now takes care of fun
A prize is now by each being won.
For anniversaries too we used to gather
Rain or shine, that didn't matter.
As time did pass some couldn't stay
Twas Mabel first who moved away.

Grandma Mueller was called in fifty-three
Then Oma next, got sick you see.
Frieda's gone since fifty-five
And Anna Sprenger in sixty died.

With Katie gone since sixty-eight

It leaves just seven of the originate
Of course a few have been added to
Who took their place, first one then two.

Twas Alice first, she moved away
Then Clara and Irmy -no more are they-
Because of illness now Rose begs leave
We hope soon back her we'll receive.

Our Elsa dear, is now getting old;
She will be eighty- we are told.
No longer a member she is able to be
But as a guest we hope her often to see.

This leaves as charters just us few
Just Lydia, Irene and Muellers two
And Norma of course, and added there be
Minnie and Mildred and Florence – these three.

Millersville Fire Department

In 1923, a fire broke out at the Rudolph Schorer residence right in the middle of the village. Village people managed to put out the fire with small fire extinguishers and pails of water. The village needed fire protection. On January 24, 1923, twenty-six village men met for the purpose of organizing a volunteer fire department. A constitution and by-laws were drawn for the Millersville volunteer fire department and officers elected as follows: Adolph Bohlmann, president; Rudolph Schorer, vice-president; Alfred Bitter, secretary-treasurer; William Prigge and Gust Wiedmeyer, directors.

Financial help was needed, so a membership drive was organized and by the end of the year 46 members were acquired. To further offset their financial problems, they decided to have a picnic and parade. So the first of many parades was held in the summer of 1924, followed by a picnic in the school grounds.

In 1928 a cistern, 20 feet in diameter and 14 feet deep and fed by a nearby well was built next to the village store.

It was then that they had their first public card party and have since sponsored a card party every spring and fall.

In the year 1929 an electric alarm was installed at the firehouse with the addition of a new Peter Pirsch 500 gallon fire truck. In 1931 a dam was built and a string of tiles from the Pigeon River to Fischers Creek was laid for more abundant storage of water.

During the years of 1931-1933 the Millersville Fire Department averaged 25 fires and runs per year. The department became a corporation in 1941. Its first officers were Adolph Kaemmer, president; Fred Sprenger, vice president; Otto Griebe, secretary; Henry Mueller Jr, fire chief. At the first meeting following their incorporation they proposed a plan for a Firemen's Park, and a six acre tract of land along the Pigeon River was purchased from Ray Bitter. It was leveled and graded, water was piped, trees were planted and a gravel driveway made. The dedication of the new park took place at their annual picnic July 12, 1942.

In 1952 the fire department purchased an additional 60 foot frontage. In January of 1954 a special meeting was called in regards to the building of a new fire house. Firemen attending the meeting expressed their wishes in obtaining a new fire house at a reasonable cost. On May 22, 1955 the fire department had its opening of the new firehouse, which was built large enough to accommodate three trucks and with a large room in the rear to be used for meetings and other events.

In February, 1959 the board of directors called a special meeting in regards to the acquiring a used truck with a large tank for the purpose of transporting water to the site of the fire runs, to which the department had been called, for it was found that the rural departments were so often handicapped by the

1946 Chev. - 600 gal. tank 500 gpm pump

lack of water, the board agreed that the need was great, and approved the purchase of the 1,500 gallon tanker which was acquired in February of the same year.

In 1979, the Millersville and Howards Grove Fire Departments merged, but still kept their separate stations. By 1990 the two stations were sold and the village of Howards Grove built a new station and leased it to the fire department. The location of this new 8000 square foot building was built in the middle of the village on South Wisconsin Drive.

July 11, 1950
Sheboygan Press

Advertisement- Firemen's Picnic and Village Centennial at Millersville July 15-16! Free slides of old time pictures up to 100 years old will be shown on screen. Be sure to see these picures! You may see yourself, relatives or friends from pictures taken over 50 years ago. Open air dancing Saturday, with music by Kenny Olm's Orchestra. Big parade at one o'clock Sunday, featuring old time floats and dresses and modern equipment. Free attractions by Lou Hols! Enjoy yourself at Millersville July 15-16.

August 10, 1959
Sheboygan Press
Millersville Firemen Complete Study Course

Completing a 10-week course in firefighting-Fire Service Practices for Volunteer Fire Departments were members of the Millersville Volunteer Fire Department Monday night. From left to right, first row, they are: Fire Chief Lester Sprenger, Gerhardt Mueller, second assistant chief; Arno H. Wangemann, Sheboygan, the instructor; Reuben Hoppe, Donald Mueller, Norman Spindler Jr., Eugene Hickmann, Leroy Valenstein, Al Bitter Jr.and Martin Grunewald Jr. Back row: George Sprenger, Gilbert Klein, Harvey Schorer, Walter Schneider, Robert Spindler, secretary-treasurer, and Milton Sebald.

The training dealt with forcible entry practices, rope, hose and fire stream practices, ventilation, apparatus and rescue practices. This training course was taught by the State Board of Vocational and Adult Instruction, Madison and jointly sponsored by the Sheboygan Vocational School.

Howards Grove Fire Department as seen in 2008

Howards Grove First Responders

Officially August 1, 1984, the Howards Grove First Responder Unit began. Although in 1982, it started on a small scale until financial help could be obtained. Backing came from the EMS and financial support from the village, township, the local Lions Club, VFW, Jaycettes and Aid Association for Lutherans organization.

When arriving at a call the responders basically take charge of the situation. In the case of heart attacks, strokes, accidents, etc. they perform CPR, stop bleeding and administer oxygen. The responders can arrive at a scene in Howards Grove within two minutes. It would take an ambulance fifteen to twenty minutes to arrive from Sheboygan.

Within the first eight months twenty-one emergency calls were answered. All the responders are very dedicated people. Two members are on call daily, 24 hours a day and 365 days a year. The community is very supportive and proud of their service.

Millersville Parades and Picnics

Picnics and parades were popular fundraisers for the fire department. Each parade would start at the Millersville Box Company and end up at the school grounds. The first parade took place in 1924. Every parade had a theme and most men, women and children participated. The Millersville picnics and parades became well-known and drew enormous crowds.

Otto Sprenger lead most of the Millersville parades with his stallions side-stepping all the way.

Floats and participants would arrive early at the Millersville Box Company yard on parade day, line up and once the parade commenced would proceed west toward the Mueller farm land with Otto Sprenger leading the way on one of his stallions. The parade would proceed north on the farm lane leading up to the woods and then turn east again back toward the Box Company. Picnics were held at the Millersville School ground until 1941. After the Millersville Fire Department incorporated it purchased a six-acre tract of land adjoining the Pigeon River from Raymond Bitter and further picnics were held in that park. No picnics were held during the WWII years.

From Elmer Koppelmann's book, *Howards Grove, Wisconsin-*

> The commitment to hold a firemen's picnic meant that everyone in the community had to do what they could to help. It was almost impossible to achieve success without everyone's cooperation.

> The Millersville Firemen's Picnic of 1952 was destined to stand out in the minds of village residents. Held on the 19th and 20th of July it was greatly affected by the deluge of rain that drenched the entire county on Saturday night. Violet Usadel remembers that the picnic was moved out of the park and set up on the street just outside her front door.

Elmer Pieper recalled, "We had the picnic Saturday night. The sky was getting blacker and it was lightning like hell. My wife was working in the cheese stand, and I was working the bratwurst stand, and I said to her, 'Let's go home.' We didn't have the warnings like we have today, and we went home as it started to rain and storm.

We went to bed and after a while the fire siren went off. When I got outside I could see the entire flats were under water. When I got to the firehouse everything was there, but no guys, so I went down to the picnic grounds, and the water in the picnic grounds was over three feet deep and everything was floating away.

We had beer and soda and food in the stands that we left there overnight. We had a couple of guys who stayed through the night to watch in a little shack. Suddenly water was coming in the front door of the shack, but quickly we were sitting in water.

Frederick Sprenger, with a tractor and hay rack, and all the firemen worked to get everything to higher ground. I had to go home to help my father with the milking and after that we set the whole thing up in the town. We were all flat, but we had no sleep. The guys didn't go home, but they worked straight through Sunday night. Then people got stuck in the parking lot and Millersville Box had a small caterpillar that they used to pull people out.

That picnic I will never forget."

1951 Millersville Picnic- When the Millersville Park flooded, firemen fought rising water and moved their stands onto the dry ground of Millersville Avenue. Seen above: 1. Bob Larson, 2. Lynne Usadel, 3. Beverly Larson, 4. Harold Usadel, 5. Harry Erbstoeszer, 6. Violet Usadel and 7. Margaret Goedeke.

August 23, 1934
Sheboygan County News
Millersville

The Millersville Volunteer Fire Department held its annual picnic at the School Park here on Sunday, August 19. People from all over the neighboring counties attended. The village proper and the road sides from east to west were packed with people when the parade passed at one o'clock. Otto Sprenger on his favorite stallion carrying our flag led the parade. The thirty-piece Brillion Band in uniform was followed by the fire trucks from Millersville, Howards Grove and Ada. The many beautiful floats and processions were as follows: Bitter-Neumann and Company float, Millersville Cheese float by N. Dassow, Otto Sprenger Tavern float, The Midget Barber Shop float by Otto Schneider, a miniature barn sponsored and made by Gust. Wiedmeyer, and the Millersville Box Company, Henry Berth Garage Eskimo float of Alaska, the four floats of the seasons, spring, summer, fall and winter by the ladies of the village, Rock Garden float sponsored by O. Heusterberg, Where Many A Happy Hour is Spent, a shanty belonging to the Buck Fever Patience Club, decorated bicycles; a small rig with pups and children; a few ponies; a group of nurses in white uniforms and Sun Bonnet Girls in green and pink. A very beautiful float sponsored by the Howards Grove Bank; a float in orange by H.C. Burhop; Howards Grove Meat market; Monterey Tavern; Summer Garden's float; Euneva Cigars; Knuth and Kuester's model car; a beautiful float From Holland by A. Kleinhans of Plymouth; a float with miniature car by Ted's Garage of Sheboygan; a truck of horses by Louis Mayer and son, and also one by Kleinhans and Simonsmeier of Plymouth; several horses sponsored by Mr. Hemb; trucks from Sheboygan Baking Company, Muhs, Diamond Products, Grasse Oil, Truttschel's Service Station Float from Sheboygan; five small rigs representing crops; straw and cedar trimmed carts; A Century of Progress cart; a donkey and various other comic processions. Everyone gathered in the school ground park where refreshments and concessions of all sorts were had. The Brillion Band with its popular and old-time selections furnished musical entertainment for the afternoon and evening. After 8 o'clock Romy Gosz and his orchestra furnished music and the large open-air dance space was packed with dancers. It is believed that this year's picnic proved the very largest attendance and success.

August 10, 1936
Sheboygan County News
Everyone here is busily preparing for the annual fireman's picnic which will be held again on Sunday at the school park. A special attraction by the Bavarian Schuhplatter Club will be held at 1:30pm and throughout the afternoon. The Marine Band of Manitowoc will again furnish musical entertainment for the afternoon. A large open air dance floor will be erected. Dancing will be free in the afternoon. The South Side Recording Orchestra will furnish dance music for the evening. Various raffles and concessions will be had and all refreshments will be served.

August 15, 1937
Sheboygan Press
Picnic Enjoyed By Millersville Fire Department
A large crowd thronged to the Millersville district school grounds Sunday for the annual picnic sponsored by the Volunteer Millersville firemen and thoroughly enjoyed the many games, contests, concessions and musical entertainment that was offered during the day.

A highlight of the day's picnic program was the show put on twice, once in the afternoon and once in the evening by the Cripple Creek Serenaders of WHBL.

Albert Oetling is president of the Volunteer Firemen of Millersville. The committee assisting him in charge of the picnic activities consisted of Fred Sprenger, Roland Bauman, Emil Klemme, Otto Scheibe, Adolph Kaemmer and Henry Berth.

August 26, 1940
Sheboygan County News

The Millersville Volunteer Fire Department had their annual picnic Sunday in spite of all the rain. Bratwurst and refreshments were had throughout the day and games and concessions were enjoyed by a large crowd of people. Shelter was found in Al Doro's hall and everyone reported an enjoyable time. There was, of course, no parade as scheduled for one o'clock, although many braved the rain to see it. Relatives and friends from farther away came again to partake, and the firemen were pleased as it proved successful despite the rain. Music by loud speaker and phonograph and Orthophonic was enjoyed instead of that of the 30-piece Brillion band which was to have led the parade and furnished the musical entertainment.

The ladies of the village will be busy today untrimming all the beautiful floats they took such pains with decorating for the parade postponed from last Sunday until this past Sunday which was rained out both times. Among the various ones decorated was the Bitter-Neumann float, Millersville Box Company floats, Al Doro's Tavern-a miniature tavern, The Village Choir having a real organ and choir, The Playmates float by the little girls of the village with a real cellar door, rain barrel, and yes, even apple tree, The Melody Float in white with black notes; the Milliner Salon float, American Float in national colors, and another beautiful float made by the ladies of the village also the Millersville Garage float.

Sheboygan County News
Huge Crowd Views Parade at Millersville
Rain Puts Stop to Evening Festivities at Park

An enormous crowd again packed the village street here Sunday for the annual volunteer firemen's picnic held at the school park grounds. Friends from far and near came to see the grand one o'clock parade led by Otto Sprenger on his favorite stallion and including other steeds and ponies, the fife and drum corps and Boy Scouts of Sheboygan, Millersville, Howards Grove and Ada fire trucks, many lovely and colorful floats, among which were:

The Dairy Queen- in yellow and white, by girls of the village.

May Pole- In rainbow colors by the little girls.

Wedding Float- In yellow and orange, made by the matrons of the village.

Beauty Salon- In blue and white by the Junior girls.

Harvest-In brown, orange and yellow.

Sports- In green and white.

Taxi-For the Old Maids.

Carload of Gypsies- all by the young ladies of the village.

The Model Kitchen- By Bitter-Neumann.

Patriotic Colored Float-by Millersville Box Company.

Covered Wagon- By Schneider's Barber Shop.

Al Doro's Tavern-Float.

Beautiful Float by Howards Grove State Bank.

Golden Lantern Float.

Other beer garden floats by the Box Company, Art Kraemer's tavern, Janke's Euneva float, Millersville Garage and others, Thomas Repair Shop, a large float by Jung Beer, Louis Mayer and son, tractors, rigs, comics, clowns and other participants.

The parade lined up at the mill yard, proceeded west through the village, turned in Mueller's field and returned east again back to the mill. During the afternoon drills were given by the Boy Scouts, musical entertainment furnished by Quirin Kohlbeck and his orchestra of Two Rivers to which dancing on a large open air floor was enjoyed.

Concessions, bratwurst, beer and all other refreshments were had throughout the park. Rain showers forced the large crowd to scatter and by evening the outdoor dance was impossible, thus abruptly ending another successful event in Millersville history.

Millersville Parades

1920s
Millersville Avenue, Box Company Entrance

Parade Floats
Late 1920s

Millersville Avenue Fire House in background

Millersville Fire Department

1920s   Millersville Bus Goes Where? From Here to There

1920s
Vote for Prohibition
and Get Moonshine

Milton Wiedemeyer
& Harold Usadel

Al Bitter General Merchandise

1930s

Japan –
Olga Neumann and Viola Herzog, Margaret Bitter, LaVern Herzog & Marcella Neumann

Ella Pieper, Linda Pieper, Elsa Kruse, Frieda Sprenger, Lydia Sprenger

Rose Sprenger, Irene Sebald, Florence Muetzelberg, Loraine Laack, Bernice Thomson

About 1934

Spring — Olga Neumann on left and Viola Herzog on right

Summer

Winter Eskimo Float
Otto Pieper, Katie Schorer, Rosa Boeldt,

Above: Fall
At left: Otto's Barber Shop, Left to Right: Myrtle Schneider, Roger Doro

1940

Bitter Neumann and Company
Norman Klemme

This is no bull. The parade iscoming
Gerhard Herzog

Russell Boeldt & Elroy Grunewald

Donald Bitter & Arline Sprenger Hoppe

Al's Tavern
Shirley Herzog, Carl & Edward Miller

1951 Millersville Picnic

(park was flooded)

1. Bob Larson, 2. Lynne Usadel, 3. Beverly Larson, 4. Harold Usadel, 5. Harry Erbstoeszer, 6. Violet Usadel and 7. Margaret Goedeke

L to R: Alan Sprenger, _____, Janice Reseburg, Dale Sprenger, Lynne Sprenger

Richard Pieper & Lu Ann Baumann

David Hoppe, Ken Thompson and Eugene Sebald

In the Military

Sheboygan Press
1943

Private George A. Sprenger of Millersville has been transferred and his address is now 36830044 842nd Ord. Depot, Co. 310 Ord. Bn. Camp Hood, Texas. In a recent letter he wrote that he plays shortstop on the baseball team there on Monday nights and Saturday afternoons. He also writes that he is not far from Pvt. William Prigge, another Millersville resident, stationed at Waco, Texas.

1943

Mrs. and Mrs. William Prigge received word on Thursday from their son, Staff Sergeant Henry Prigge, announcing the birth of a son that day at Scott Field, Illinois.

Pfc. Wilbert Janke Answers Nazi With Burst from Rifle
With U.S. First Army (AP)

Troops of the 83rd Division helped to blunt the tip of the German break-through thrust into Belgium and now are biting back into the enemy bulge on the First Army front. During action the night of December 28, Pfc. Wilbert Janke of Sheboygan, Wisconsin who speaks a smattering of German, answered a German's shouted demand for surrender with a burst from his automatic rifle. "There was plenty of shooting and killing," said Janke. "But the Germans, not us, were on the receiving end." Pfc. Janke is the son of Mrs. Gust. Wiedmeyer of Millersville. He was wounded in action on July 1, 1944 in France. Pfc. Janke was inducted into the service on December 28, 1942 and after several months of training with the paratroopers he was transferred to Camp Breckenridge, Ky. because of an injury to his knee. In March, 1944, he was sent overseas.

January, 1945
Pfc. Janke is Wounded Belgium

Millersville- Mrs. Gust Wiedemeyer received a telegram from the war department Friday informing her that her son, Pfc. Wilbert P. Janke, was seriously wounded in action on January 15, in Belgium and that his mail address would follow direct from the hospital where he is now confined together with details of his injuries.

Pfc. Janke was previously wounded in action in France on July 11, 1944 and was awarded the Purple Heart at that time. He had recovered and gone back into action and recently a notice was received that he had remained unharmed while standing in the street in Rochefort, Belgium calling to the German soldiers in their own language to surrender to the Americans.

He had been answered at that time with a hail of bullets cutting a slash in his trousers. Pfc. Janke entered service on December 28, 1942 and since March, 1944 has served with an Infantry unit overseas.

November 15, 1945
Millersville- Corp. Elroy Kalk returned home over the weekend to his parents, Mr. and Mrs. Richard Kalk, from the southwest Pacific area. He has an honorable discharge.

Pvt. Melvin Laack of Texas is spending a few days here with his wife and sons, Bobby and Jimmy.

1945
Pfc. Norman Klein Reported Wounded
Millersville

John Klein of this village received word last week that his son, Pfc. Norman W. Klein, was slightly wounded in action on September 14 in Italy. Pfc. Klein entered service May 25, 1942 and received his infantry training at Camp Shelby, Mississippi. Later he was transferred to Shreveport, La. and went on maneuvers at the desert training center in California. From there he went to Fort Dix, New Jersey and then overseas in December 1943 spending Christmas and New Year's aboard ship.

He arrived safely in North Africa and later was sent to Italy, where he took part in the Rome campaign. He visited at home on furlough in November, 1943.

The War Effort at Home During WWII

During WWII, the Red Cross conducted Home Nursing Classes at the Elsa Kruse home west of what is now Neumann Plumbing and Heating Company. Twenty women attended the first meeting. Mrs. Jerry Donohue was the Chairman of the Sheboygan County Red Cross Home Nursing Division, also speaking at the Millersville School P.T.A. in October 1943. the instructor was Mrs. Walter Eichenberger, with her assistant, Mrs. Jensen.

Women also attended Red Cross meetings every Tuesday in the upper flat at the Albert Oetling home in 1943, vacated by George and Ruth Sprenger when he was drafted into the Army. Often after the meetings, the group would go to the movies at Doro's.

September 15, 1944
Sheboygan Press
Millersville Unit of Red Cross Has An Excellent Year

The Millersville unit of the American Red Cross completed a year of service on August 19, with 15 women proudly wearing the first year's bar, representing 100 hours of work. Six women have previously received their service pin and the large cross given for 144 hours of work. The small cross for 72 hours is being worn by 18 women.

Work meetings were held every Tuesday, and with an average of 12 afternoon and 10 evening workers, 21,357 surgical dressings have been made during the past year. Sewing was done by 17 ladies, and a total of 140 baby bonnets, 90 pair of baby mittens, 70 baby saques, 50 housewives, 13 army kits, 10 bed pan covers and 5 bed jackets were made. Two ladies knitted four navy caps and two army sweaters. The highest number of hours in sewing and knitting given by any one woman totaled 70 hours; in making of surgical dressings, 305 hours. About 20 persons have attended the Blood Bank with several giving four pints, and one giving five pints.

The efforts of the local chairman, Mrs. Milton Sebald, with the assistance of the co-chairman, Mrs. Adolph Kaemmer, and the financial support of the Millersville Box Company and Bitter-Neumann Company have made this excellent service record possible.

Nursing Class Enjoys Party

Members of the Millersville Home Nursing class enjoyed a party on Monday evening at the home of Miss Elsa Kruse, in celebration of the completion of their home nursing course. They had as their guests their instructresses, Mrs. Walter Eichenberger, Sheboygan and Mrs. Jerry Donohue, county chairman of the American Red Cross Home Nursing committee, also of Sheboygan.

The latter presented the home nursing pins to the following members: the Mesdames Harvey Schorer, Milton Sebald, Adolph Kaemmer, Harvey Sprenger, William Thierfelder, Victor Thierfelder, Walter Schneider, Otto Schneider, William Prigge, Frederick Sprenger, Alfred Bitter, Walter Mueller, Henry Mueller and Arno Sprenger; and the Misses Elsa Kruse and Hilda Schneider.

A miniature Red Cross home nurse in patriotic and home nursing motif centered the long table at which a luncheon was served. Mrs. William Thierfelder was toastmistress. Features of the evening's entertainment included: the class song, composed by Mrs. Alfred Bitter, and dedicated to the instructress, Mrs. Eichenberger; a comedy skit, "Through the Day With the Patient in Pre-home Nursing Days", a monologue; and appropriate sayings and songs.

In expressions of appreciation, the class group remembered Mrs. Eichenberger, and the hostess, Miss Kruse, at whose home the classes had been held, with lovely gifts.

As part of the home nursing school a catchy tune was written describing the activities of the group. It was sung to the tune of In the Shade of the Old Apple Tree. It follows:

Verse 1. We have finished our Home Nursing School and will try to remember each rule. We know just what to do. When Dad gets the flu. Or the children come home sick from school.

Verse 2. How to make up their beds we all know. Give them baths from their head to their toe. Take pulse, temps, respiration. For the Doc's information. A chart with their record will show.

Verse 3. How when one has a cold in the chest. We all know mustard plaster is best. For sore elbows or heel. We make some cotton wheels. And can put up a comfy back rest.

Verse 4. Should the stork beat the Dr. some day. We can help the new babe on its way.

Our lessons we've had, How to sterilize pads. And can fix up a pleasing food tray.

Verse 5. We all liked our instructor so well, To our questions the answers she'd tell.

Teaching home care was her aim. If we fail, we're to blame. We all thank her and think she was swell.

Verse 6. We'll be missing these classes with you. But are all mighty glad we are thru.

When we need comfy feet, Sometime we may meet, Best wishes for good health to you.

Millersville Family Active in War Work
Sheboygan Press
August 27, 1942

Millersville-

The Millersville fire department has discontinued its annual picnic for the duration of the war so that food, gas and tires may be saved for the war effort. That's a sample of the patriotic spirit shown by 142 residents of Millersville. Every family in the village boasts a victory garden, and many individuals work long hours helping on the surrounding farms.

About $10,000 worth of bonds has been purchased by the village thus far. Alfred Bitter has been a leader in the sale of bonds and stamps. He is ably assisted by the school children who thus far have bought $412.95 worth of stamps.

The children have also been active in salvage work, and thus far gleaned several tons of scrap metal. The villagers have contributed approximately two tons of waste rubber and a generous portion of waste kitchen fats used in the making of glycerin in explosives.

In a drive by the United War Chest… the district in which Millersville is located went far above its quota. Backing the drive were Emil Klemme, Henry F. Mueller, Martin Boeldt and Arwin Herzog.

Over $21 was received from the village people in the USO drive.

A Morale Booster
Sheboygan Press
January 5, 1943

Patriotic Hen Does Her Bit On Food Situation

Millersville- Increased war production has become the patriotic duty of every good American citizen—yes, even every good American chicken, and to vouch for that is one proud hen at the August Millert farm, one mile north of Mohrsville in the town of Sheboygan Falls.

It seems that the other day Mrs. Millert was going around picking up the day's efforts of her flock when she came to this particularly patriotic chicken. There she found to her amazement an egg larger than a goose egg, sitting proudly in the nest. However, her surprise was just beginning, since upon opening it she found not only two unbroken yolks, but there was a third oversized egg with shell and all.

The chicken has yet to reveal its production secret to the rest of the flock.

More in the Military
1953

R.M.S.M. Herman Kuether Jr. of Charlestown, S.C. is here on leave with his parents. The Rev. and Mrs. H.A. Kuether. Seaman Kuether was on board the U.S.S. Ault of Norfork, Va. And will return to South Carolina by June 24.

1953

Pvt. Alfred Bitter Jr. is spending a week's furlough here with his parents, Mr. and Mrs. Alfred Bitter, who motored to Chicago, Saturday to call for him. He is stationed at Camp Chaffee, Arkansas.

1954
Seaman Gordon Wuestenhagen left early Sunday morning for the Great Lakes Naval Station after having spent the past 15 days leave here with his parents, Mr. and Mrs. Hugo Wuestenhagen.

Pvt. Carl Mueller arrived home Sunday morning from Ft. Leonard Wood, Mo. for a 14-day furlough with his parents, Mr. and Mrs. Henry Mueller, and brothers, Donald and Glenn. Pvt. Mueller completed 8 weeks of basic training having left for service on July 5.

1954
Millersville

Word was received by Mr. and Mrs. Hugo Wuestenhagen that their son, Gordon, with the U.S. Navy, has been transferred to San Francisco, Calif. He had been stationed at the Great Lakes Naval Station the past months.

June 1956
S.P. Carl Mueller, son of Mr. and Mrs. Henry Mueller arrived home Monday from Fort Sheridan, Ill. having completed his two years of Army Service. Carl entered U.S. service on July 6, 1954 and received his basic training at Fort Leonard Wood, Mo. He spent about two months at Texas from where he was transferred to Baumholder, Germany. He left for overseas in November, 1954 and spent 18

months there.

Millersville
1960

Earl O. Goedeke arrived home from North Carolina Saturday, after having received an honorable discharge for three years volunteer service in the United States Marines. Earl, the son of Mr. and Mrs. Robert Goedeke, enlisted and had received his basic training at San Diego, Calif. Before being stationed in North Carolina, where he spent a year, he also had been stationed at Okinawa.

Millersville
1964

Herman A. Kuether, R.M. 3 completed a 30-day leave here with his mother, Mrs. H.A. Kuether and left again Saturday morning. He was taken to Milwaukee by his two sisters-in-laws, Mrs. Eugene Kuether of here and Mrs. Robert Kuether of Sheboygan. He took a plane from Mitchell Airfield to Flint, Michigan where he visited over Sunday with Jim Hesling. From there he left on Monday to report back to New Jersey. He had been called home from Germany where he was stationed by the death of his father, the Rev. H.A. Kuether. Because relatives came from various distances to attend funeral service he was able to meet them all, especially his three sisters and families; Mrs. Lawrence (Ruth) Fischer, Beaver Dam, Mrs. Harold (Doris) Fischer and Mrs. Howard (Vera) Williams both of Cedar Rapids, Iowa. He visited here with his sister, Mrs. Milford (Irene) Henning and his three brothers, Richard, Robert and Eugene and their respective families also.

Millersville
June 14, 1965

Pvt. Gerald Schmidt left again for Fort Leonard Wood, Mo., after spending a leave here with his parents, Mr. and Mrs. Marvin Schmidt.

Millersville
July 27, 1965

Pvt. Steve Sprenger, having recently completed his basic training at fort Knox, Ky. Is spending a leave here with his parents, Mr. and Mrs. Frederick Sprenger.

Millersville
1967

Sp.-4 Glenn Mueller is home after receiving his discharge from the Army. He had been stationed the past year in Vietnam. His mother, Mrs. Henry Mueller, accompanied Mr. and Mrs. Donald Mueller and son, Dean, and Mr. and Mrs. Lester Sprenger to Chicago to meet him at the airport.

1968

Major Keith Kuester has arrived from Vietnam, where he had been the past year, at the home of his parents, Mr. and Mrs. Walter Kuester. His wife and sons, Michael, Eric and Gerard arrived here to meet him on Sunday from Nancy, France, where they lived during his absence. Gerard was born there in January and met his father and grandparents for the first time. They will leave for The Hague, Holland, in several weeks where the major will be an advisor to the Dutch Air force for the next three years.

Weekly Life in a Small Village

Each week, or sometimes every other week the local correspondents to the Sheboygan and Plymouth papers would report on what transpired in their respective village the previous week.

Mrs. Kaemmer, who covered Millersville, and Mrs. Karstadt, who wrote about Howards Grove, captured the flavor of life in a small village.

If any person in the village did anything that was in any way noteworthy these correspondents were sure to write about it in their next column.

Special occasions were generally covered in detail as were the comings and goings of individual families in the village.

If someone would collect each of the columns for a number of years, it would be possible to tell, among other things, the social structure of the village as well as the relationships among the people mentioned in the columns.

Following are reprints two of the columns as published to give you an idea of what life in a small village was like at two different points in history.

The first was written by Mrs. Karstedt and appeared in the 7 June 1935 edition of the *Sheboygan Press* :

> Mrs. Ray Wagner was hostess to the members of her sheepshead club at her home on Tuesday evening. Scorers were; Mrs. Herman Karstedt, Miss Lucy Frome, Mrs. Lena Karstedt, and Miss Laura Schnette. At 10:30 a delicious repast was served.
>
> Mr. and Mrs. Clarence Kolb and daughter, Beverly, of Cleveland, Mr. and Mrs. Walter Lautenschlaeger and children, Frederick and Enola, of Sheboygan, Mr. and Mrs. Henry Sommer and Miss Esther Sommer were Sunday dinner and supper guests of Mr. and Mrs. Gaylord Karstedt.
>
> Mrs. Rudolph Usadel is well on the way to recovery after being ill for the past week.
>
> Mrs. Otto Oetling is still confined to her bed by illness. Her many friends wish her a rapid recovery.
>
> Mr. and Mrs. Roland Neumann entertained relatives and friends at their home on Sunday evening in honor of the former's birthday. Cards furnished amusement for the evening and at 10:30 a delicious repast was served to the following guests: Mr. and Mrs. Norman Klemme and daughter, Dolores, Mr. and Mrs. Adolph Kaemmer and daughter, Alleen, Mr. and Mrs. Gerhardt Herzog and daughter, LaVerne, Mr. and Mrs. Harvey Schorer, Mr. and Mrs. Henry Mueller Jr., Mr. and Mrs. Alfred Doro and sons, Roger and James, Mr. and Mrs. George Neumann and daughter, June, and Christ Neumann.
>
> Mr. and Mrs. George Pippert and family were Memorial Day guests of Mr. and Mrs. B. Hartmann of Milwaukee. While at Milwaukee, Mrs. Pippert suddenly took ill and had to remain until Tuesday when she returned to her home.
>
> Misses Violet Erbstoeser, Alvira Grunwald and Esther Paul, Harold Usadel, and Frederick Huesterberg motored to Madison on Sunday where they visited with Frederick Sprenger, who is a student at the University of Wisconsin. Mr. and Mrs. Al Karstedt of Sheboygan were Sunday guests of Mrs. Lena Karstedt and Mr. and Mrs. Walter Karstedt.
>
> Mrs. H. Kaestner spent Memorial Day with Mrs. Henry Klemme of Kiel.
>
> Henry Bitter of Michigan was a guest on Sunday and Monday with Mr. and Mrs. Alfred Bitter.
>
> Mr. and Mrs. Otto Bramstedt and Mr. and Mrs. Helmuth Bramstedt, all of Fond du Lac, were Sunday guests of Mr. and Mrs. Otto Sprenger

Mr. and Mrs. William Prigge, Miss Gertrude Prigge, and Gerhardt Prigge, Mrs. Ernst Wuestenhagen and Mr. and Mrs. Hugo Wuestenhagen motored to Waukesha on Saturday to attend the funeral of Mrs. William Bahr. Mrs. Bahr was formerly Miss Annie Prigge.

Arline Sprenger, daughter of Mr. and Mrs. Arwin Sprenger, has returned to her home here after being confined a day to a hospital in Sheboygan where doctors removed a tumor from her neck.

Mr. and Mrs. Louis Herzog of Reedsville spent Sunday as guests with Mr. and Mrs. John Henning.

William Thierfelder Jr., of Milwaukee has charge of the German school near Millersville which began on Monday, June 3.

Mr. and Mrs. William Schuette entertained relatives and friends at their home on Monday evening in honor of the former's birthday. Sheepshead was played and scorers were Theodore Truttschel, Mrs. Norman Klemme and Dr. Albert Stolzmann. At 10:30 refreshments were served.

The second was written by Mrs. Kaemmer and appeared in the *Sheboygan Press* on 12 April 1951:

Millersville---The quarterly meeting of St. Paul's Lutheran congregation here was held Sunday after divine services at the church school auditorium.

Mrs. William Thierfelder was taken to Memorial Hospital on Monday.

Mrs. Walter Rau had surgery at St. Nicholas hospital on Thursday.

Mr. and Mrs. William Prigge returned home on Saturday from Tempe, Arizona, where they had been visiting the past two weeks with their son and wife, Prof. and Mrs. William Prigge.

Private First Class and Mrs. Donald Mueller of (A.F.B.) Camp Fairchild, Wash., were callers Thursday of Mr. and Mrs. Elmer Pieper.

Arwin and Arno Sprenger and Karl Muetzelburg spent Monday at Chicago. The former returned home while the later two motored on to Illinois.

Millersville area residents to receive new *Press* Want Ad service. Mrs. Adolph Kaemmer has been appointed the official *Sheboygan Press* Want Ad taker for your area. It's so easy to place an ad through Mrs. Kaemmer---just call Mosel 45 3S.

Mr. and Mrs. George Sprenger entertained on Saturday in honor of their son Dale's second birthday anniversary. Guests from away were Mr. and Mrs. Henry Schueffner of near Kohler.

Relatives helped Mrs. Milton Sebald observe her birthday anniversary on Thursday evening.

Alfred Bitter, Jr., And Donald Kuester of Watertown, spent the week here with the Alfred Bitter family.

Mr. and Mrs. Harvey Schorer accompanied her nephew and sisters, Kenneth Olm, Mrs. Ferdy Olm, and Mr. and Mrs. Arno Hansmann of Spring Valley and Mrs. Roland Fiedler of Cleveland to Milwaukee on Thursday where they spent the day.

Mr. and Mrs. Martin Boeldt, Mrs. Harvey Sprenger, Mrs. Arno Sprenger, Mrs. Lillie Boeldt, and Mrs. William Thierfelder attended funeral services for the former's cousin, Henry Jochmann at Kiel on Thursday.

Mrs. Mabel Baldwin, Mr. and Mrs. Milton Schmidt and family of Kohler, were Sunday supper guests of Mrs. Hilda Schneider and father, Ed. Schneider

Patricia Sprenger spent a few days at the Art Knuth home near Johnsonville.

Mr. and Mrs. Harold Braun and Dennis of Howards Grove visited last Thursday evening with Mr. and Mrs. Nelson Kuhn.

Millersville Farm Institute held at Doro's Hall

Millersville Businessmen Hold Institute

Quality of hay and silage samples supplied by Sheboygan County farmers at the Millersville Farm Institute on Friday is discussed by J. W. Crowley (center) following afternoon session at Doro's Hall. Left to right are: Arthur Athorp, Roland Schomberg, Jake LeMahieu, Mr. Crowley, Henry Johanning, Edmund Schulz and Ray Bimmel.—(Sheboygan Press photo.)

February 27, 1953

The local Farmers' Institute was led each year by the County Agricultural Agent from the University of Wisconsin Extension Office. The Farmers' Institute was a day of education designed to bring farmers up-to-date on the latest crop problems and solutions and dairy innovations. It was a great place to network and meet friends. The day ran from 10 a.m. to 3 p.m. and was held annually. It usually took place in the spring of the year, February or March before fieldwork began for the year.

A lunch was then served by the ladies of the businessmen of the village.

That's Water, Not Oil
1949

No Shortage of Water In Millersville

There's no water shortage at Arwin Sprenger home in Millersville.

In fact, there was altogether too much water Friday and Saturday as a well-drilling crew tapped an underground reservoir of water under pressure and unleashed a geyser that spouted 15 feet into the air.

The resulting flood was more than the Sprengers had bargained for, but the crew capped the well and by Saturday had the necessary fittings in place to pipe water into the Sprenger home and to the adjoining Millersville Box factory of which Mr. Sprenger is treasurer and manager.

The Millersville fire department brought its truck to the scene Friday and discovered that the truck, pumping 500 gallons per minute couldn't keep up with the flow from the well. After the well was cleaned Saturday, the flow increased to an estimated 1,000 gallons per minute.

Pressure was great enough to raise water in a vertical pipe to a point 30 feet above ground level. Mr. Sprenger said the well probably would be used in the fire protection set-up at the box factory. The Sprengers had the new well drilled when their old 46-foot well proved inadequate. The new well was drilled to a depth of 166 feet.

Daily Life in Millersville

Sheboygan Press
February 22, 1923

Howards Grove and Millersville have electric lights in their homes, their factories and their schools, something they have not been able to boast in their history. And it is probable that in the future, not far distant, they will have electric power with which to operate their factories and for other uses to which they see fit to put it.

Millersville people celebrated the event last evening with a program of public festivities. While there was no special program in Howards Grove, the occasion was celebrated almost as extensively as if there had been one, as everyone was present when the lights were turned on.

Sheboygan County News
August, 1934

Miss Bernice Sprenger of the area played the part of *Little Boy Blue* in the *Superba* staged at the county fair on Tuesday and Wednesday evenings. Her parents, Mr. and Mrs. Arwin Sprenger, witnessed the play on Tuesday evening.

Sheboygan County News
January 17, 1934
Renk's Circus Review was playing here since Friday, January 4.

Sheboygan County News
December 13, 1934

Everyone from this vicinity attended the tenth wedding anniversary dance of Mr. and Mrs. Arwin Herzog of here which was held a John Kuylen's hall, Edwards, Saturday evening. Music was furnished by Quirin Kolbeck's orchestra.

Mr. and Mrs. Louis Herzog, Jr. and sons of Manitowoc, Mr. and Mrs. Walter Herzog and the latter's sisters of Reedsville came to attend the wedding dance of the former's brother and sister-in-law, Mr. and Mrs. Arwin Herzog.

Sheboygan County News
October 31, 1935

The Hanneman Players who have been entertaining at Otto Sprenger's hall here the past week featured an amateur talent program on Sunday evening. People came from distant vicinities and the hall was filled to capacity. Fourteen contestants partook. Mr. and Mrs. Milton Schneider of Millhome, who sang a tenor and alto duet to guitar and mandolin accompaniments won first place; Miss Ruby Huesterberg of her won second place on her harmonica and guitar selections and John Kolb and Raymond Lutze of Edwards, playing piano accordion and concertina, won the third prize. The judges appointed by the audience were Miss Edna Hehling, Mrs. Karl Muetzelberg and Arwin Herzog, all of here.

(Millersville had its resident entertainers in the 1930s. Sisters, Ruby and Adela Heusterberg played the guitar and mandolin respectively. The duo sang and yodeled. Milton and Wilhelmina Schneider sang and played guitar. Merlin Rautman sang *Rainbow Around My Shoulder*. Another fun entertainment occurred when candy was also sold; the wrappers were saved by the boys and given to girls of their choice. The girls that collected the most wrappers won a prize.)

Plymouth Post
March 7, 1901

Emma Sprenger-later Mrs. Otto Pieper- 13 year old daughter of William Sprenger of Town Herman lost her right arm when she got caught in the horse-power machine while cutting feed. She is under doctor's care and her condition is favorable even though she lost her right arm.

June 10, 1937
Sheboygan Press
Automobile Thief Escapes from Millersville Man

Driving a stolen automobile, a thief, after asking that his automobile be filled with gas, Wednesday night drove away from a Millersville garage, without paying for the purchase with Milton Dickmann, attendant, hanging on to the car until he was shoved off onto the road. Mr. Dickmann said he rolled over several times, but was not injured.

Police believe the thief was driving an automobile stolen earlier in the evening from in front of 1526 Indiana Avenue. The vehicle belongs to Elmer Herr, 1512 Indiana Avenue.

Authorities are of the impression that the several car thefts perpetrated in Sheboygan recently have been the work of one man. They also believe that with the arrest of this person some of the hold-ups which have been staged in the city and county will be cleared up.

Plates Always Missing
The automobiles are usually recovered a day or so after they have been stolen and the license plates are always missing.

Mr. Dickmann told sheriff's deputies that the man asked for gas and left his motor running. After filling the tank he went to the window of the automobile where the man was sitting to get his money. The man threw the car in gear and started away with Mr. Dickmann hanging on to the side. Grasping for the wheel of the vehicle, Mr. Dickmann attempted to steer it into an elm tree. The driver kept punching and prodding him as the car gained speed until he was thrown onto the road.

Sheboygan County News
May 23, 1938

Frederick Heusterberg was pleasantly surprised at his home Wednesday evening, the occasion being his twenty-first birthday. Cards were played and prizes awarded to Mrs. Art Strassburger, Miss Anita Klemme, Mrs. Adolph Kaemmer, Miss Esther Paul and Evelyn Paul. The Misses Ruby and Adela Heusterberg entertained with guitar, mandolin and harmonica selections and song. A repast was served to about 30 guests.

Sheboygan County News
April 20, 1939

Most every one of this vicinity attended the play *The Absent-Minded Professor* given by the Alumni of Howards Grove at Monterey Hall there on Wednesday evening. The Misses Bernice Sprenger and Verna Heusterberg of here took part and the Misses Ruby and Adela Heusterberg presented special musical and vocal numbers between acts. Miss Olinda Prange coached the play which proved very successful and was enjoyed by all. So great was the crowd who came to attend, that many had to be turned away. Therefore the cast will present the play again on Friday evening, April 21st.

Sheboygan County News
Millersville

Mrs. A.E. Kaemmer
R.1. Sheboygan, Wis.

October 16, 1939

Most everyone here enjoyed the entertainment presented at Al Doro's hall this week given by the Hanneman entertainers. The show opened on Monday evening and ran until Sunday with a Popularity and Amateur Talent contest. Miss Doris Oetling was the voted the most popular lady with Miss Bernetta Illig winning second. In the amateur talent contest, Roger and James Doro of this village received second prize after having tied for first with Miss Virginia Faase and her young brother William who sang duets. Roger played the piano accordion while James played guitar and accompanied him musically. Miss Eunice Schneider also of this village won third place. She entertained on the piano accordion also. Others from this village and vicinity who took part and gave a grand performance were Orville

Knoener on his piano accordion, Donald Bitter on his violin, grouped with his two cousins, Grace and Jeanette Schneider who played Hawaiian guitar and guitar, Evangeline Winkel of near here who did a song and tap dance and John Kohl with his accordion. There were others who took part and won a prize also. At the weekly performances Mr. and Mrs. Hanneman entertained with hand tricks, comedy sketches, movie reels and puppet shows.

Trips to the Movies

On June 13, 1946, 40 people from Millersville motored to Campbellsport to Fisher's Movie House and everyone got in for free. This was part of a promotion to have movies shown on the back of Alfred Doro's barn-early outdoor movies. Merchants from the area sponsored the showing of feature films. People would bring their own chairs, sit on blankets or watch from their cars. They were shown every summer until the early part of the 1950s. As part of this trip the group then went to Bauer's Hotel to see a 700lb. man. He was Edward H. "Mush" Bauer.

Special, Fond du Lac *Commonwealth Reporter*- February 12, 1954- 780 Pound 'Mush' Bauer Shrinks to Mere 685 on Diet-

When Edward H. "Mush" Bauer Campbellsport's 780 pound bartender, entered St. Agnes Hospital recently, nurses had to place tables on either side of his bed to keep him from falling out. Bauer, suffering from a leg infection, couldn't rest comfortably on the narrow hospital bed, so he ordered his own oversize bed brought from his home and installed in the hospital room.

Mush is taking a keen interest in hospital treatments and thinks the nurses and sisters are a swell bunch. He tries to cause the as little trouble as possible, but the other night when he got out of bed to get a drink of water he fell and was unable to get up.

The nurses, who came to his assistance, found it impossible to lift him so they put in a call to the city police. With the aid of two members of the force, who rushed to the hospital, Bauer was finally restored to his bed.

Since entering the institution, Bauer has been placed on a rigid diet and has lost 95 pounds. His 86-inch waist is shrinking. He gets about 1,500 food calories a day. Bauer doesn't know how long he will have to remain in the hospital and says he doesn't care. He likes it there, but he plans to return to his hotel sample room duties (saloon) when he recovers. He is 42 years old and his weight and girth have earned him international attention.

Edward "Mush" Bauer

Millersville Recreation Association and Athletics

The first meeting of the Millersville Recreation Association was held January 21, 1938. Alfred Bitter was the first president, Fred Sprenger vice-president and August Knoener, secretary-treasurer.

Above: Dressing houses located east of the pond; one for the men and one for the women.

Below: The swimming pond with Riverside Auto in the background.

In 1937, August Knoener struck an artesian well on his property which is now 1603 South Wisconsin Drive. The continuous flow of water ran to the land next to it owned by Alfred Bitter. Mr. Bitter donated the land to the Millersville Recreation Association which decided to dig a swimming pond. Each spring the water in the pond would be drained out and the mud scraped out. Some years gravel or sand was placed in the bottom and then the pond was again filled with water, ready for a summer of swimming. It the early 1970s the liability of the pond became too great. A motion was made in 1979 to close the pool. The pond was then drained and filled with dirt.

A ball park was also built east of the pond. Still there today, it is known as Riverside Park. In the 1940s a softball fast-pitch league was sponsored by the organization. It was great entertainment for many people.

The major fundraiser for the organization was an annual Recreation Picnic which was held on the park grounds along the river. The last picnic was held in the 1960s. Later in the 1960s to early 1970s, an annual dance was held at Laack's Hall in Johnsonville.

In 1970 three young men organized a slow-pitch softball league. It was very popular and so the next year the Recreation Association took over the league. The league was limited to all village people and graduates of Howards Grove High School.

Funds became limited so they decided to host a softball tournament. The first tournament was a great success. Due to the number of teams replying throughout the county, some had to be turned away. Eventually two tournaments a year were held.

After the first tournament it became clear that the park was insufficient for functions such as this. The lighting needed to be redone; the outfield fence was a snow fence; there was no building for concessions and bathroom facilities were outhouses. It was then decided to sell the park to the village for one dollar. The village got funding to install adequate lighting and build a concession building with bathroom facilities. Eventually an announcing and score building was built and bleachers were added. The members donated most of the labor. Later a shelter was built next to the concession stand which was donated by Adrian and Adela Damrow in memory of their son, Robert.

After about twenty years, softball tournaments were being held all over the county and teams became harder to get. In the early 1990s the Recreation Association decided to hold a new fundraiser which was called "Bossy Bingo". This became a real success and the ball tournaments were dropped. On Bossy Bingo day a three on three basketball tournament is also held on the grounds for youth of all ages. Basketball courts are set up for approximately 70-80 teams. Up to 1000 people attended the event.

In 2004 the concession stand was added to accommodate sales. The concession stand now ties into the shelter.

Over the years the Millersville Recreation Association has donated several thousand dollars to the Howards Grove School System and sponsored many youth programs.

October 17, 1940

The Millersville Recreation Association held a meeting at Al Doro's place Wednesday evening. The association has contracted for a series of six weekly movies to begin November 2 at Al Doro's hall. The pictures to be shown are *Wind Jammer*, *Magnificent Obsession*, *Fit for a King*, *Last of the Mohicans*, *Rainbow on the River* and *Heaven on Earth* besides comics and other usual features. Proceeds from these evenings' entertainments will be used for the recreational fund, and a cordial welcome is extended to the public to attend.

Millersville Rec Group Holds Annual Picnic
Millersville

1954

On Sunday the Millersville Recreational Association held another annual picnic at its Millersville Firemen's Park. Refreshments, games and kiddie rides provided entertainment as did the Little German Band of Kiel. Credit for its success goes to the committee in charge- including Walter Kuester, Norman Klein, Nelson Kuhn, Harold Bitter, Ernst, Fred and George Sprenger.

The origin of this organization dates back to 1937. Because of an artesian well on the former August Knoener property-now that of Nelson Kuhn just south of the village- that started a continuous flow of water, the idea in the minds of the villagers finally found reality in the fine swimming pool that became a community project and one of Millersville's proudest achievements. Many improvements have been made and a beautiful park has resulted. Trees were planted, lawn seeded, bathhouses, diving boards, picnic benches were built, a driveway and parking space were made. A ball diamond and footlights were erected so that to date the old swimming pool is a wonderful recreation center. It has ball games besides swimming in summer and a skating rink in winter.

Sports

Millersville's Basketball Team 1920-1921

First Row: August Dedow, Walter Pieper, Manager and Gerhard Herzog; Back row: Erwin Wehrman, Adolph Kaemmer and Erwin Wuestenhagen

Sheboygan County News
January 17, 1934

The Millersville Athletics won a hard and exciting basketball game with Elkhart Lake at the Elkhart Lake High School gym on Thursday evening in an overtime game by a score of 28 to 26.

The Millersville Athletics won their first basketball game from Glenbeulah in the Amateur League on Friday evening, the score being 25 to 28. The line-up for Millersville Athletics is as follows: Ray Russart, center; Carl Harms, forward; Arno Sprenger, forward; Harold Usadel, guard; Milton Wiedemeyer, guard; Herbert Sohn, guard; and Art Bennin, guard with Adolph Kaemmer as manager. The second team won the preliminary game from Glenbeulah that evening by a score of 30 to 16. The line-up is as follows: Frederick Heusterberg, center; Norman Klein, guard; George Sprenger, guard; Henry Bennin, forward; Henry Harms, forward and Melvin Laack, forward. On Sunday afternoon both teams defeated Batavia at the Batavia hall. The Millersville Athletics won by a score of 35 to 25 and the second team won the preliminary by a score of 18 to 17.

Sheboygan County News
June 17, 1934

Millersville- The local baseball team has started the season with success. They won two games on their home diamond with the Haslee Oils and the Avenue Exchange teams of Sheboygan and have won a game with Greenbush. However, on Sunday they met defeat with the Sheboygan Falls team at Sheboygan Falls.

Sheboygan County News
August 30, 1934

Harold Usadel, Arno Sprenger, Frederick Huesterburg and George Harms of the local baseball team of here played with the Sheboygan County Amateur League All Stars vs. the Rainbow League All Stars at Plymouth on Tuesday and won by a score of 20 to 12.

Millersville is Defeated by Falls Merchants Sunday
Getting five out of their seven runs the second inning, the Falls Merchants easily defeated the Millersville entry of the Sheboygan County amateur league on Sunday at the Richardson ball park, the final score being 7 to 1.

1934-1935 Millersville Baseball Team
Kneeling: ?, Alex Russert, Ray Russert, George Harms, ?, Arno Sprenger, Adolph Kaemmer.
Seated: Henry Prigge, Harold Usadel, Earl Horneck, Harold Braun, Herb Sohn.

Andy Willadsen, star twirler of the Merchants held the Millersville team to only four hits throughout the entire tussle. A hit by Usadel, the 2nd baseman, in the first inning, gained by an error on the part of Arthur Guiltmeyer counted for the first run the Millersville team was to register in the game. Harms, third baseman, connected with a hit in the fourth frame. R. Russart, centerfielder, got on in the second inning and Kalk chalked one up in the fifth. Successive hits by E. Willadsen, Hall and Hilbert Wolfet counted for one run for the home team in the first inning and five runs in the fifth.

Sheboygan County News
March 26, 1936

A large crowd witnessed the basketball games at Howards Grove Thursday evening in which the alumni team was defeated by a score of 25 to 18 by the high school team. The high school seconds won a preliminary game from the Mission House team while the girls' team was defeated by the Waldo girls. The Misses Bernice Sprenger, Ruth Kuether, Anita Strassburger, Verna and Ruby Huesterberg and Rose Boeldt, all of this district, played the girls' team while Frederick and Arno Sprenger and Frederick Huesterberg of here played with the alumni team.

Sheboygan County News
March 29, 1936

The Millersville Old Time basketball players enjoyed a game with Howards Grove on Saturday evening. They were defeated by a score of 29-59. Those who played were: Frederick Sprenger, center; Frederick Huesterberg and Carl Harms, forwards, and Adolph Kaemmer and Harold Usadel, guards. Arno Sprenger of this village was referee. Harms and Kaemmer had for several years played on both the Millersville and Howards Grove teams.

Sheboygan County News
February 29, 1940

Mr. and Mrs. Arno Sprenger, Mr. and Mrs. Adolph Kaemmer attended the basketball game at Town Wilson when the Get-together Millersville Team defeated the Wilson team by a score of 37-19. Those who played for Millersville were: A. Sprenger, L. Sprenger, H. Bitter, C. Harms, A. Kaemmer, W. Drier and M. Boll.

Girls Softball 1945
Arline Hoppe

In 1945, a Millersville girls' softball team was organized. Oscar Meyer, who was the bookkeeper at Millersville Box Company was asked to be our coach. Our team had only two balls and a bat, probably made by Gustav Wiedmeyer.

The girls in the infield were: Arline Sprenger Hoppe, pitcher, Adela Heusterberg Damrow, catcher, Verna Huesterberg Groene, first base, Doris Oetling Goetsch, second base, Bernice Sprenger Thompson, short stop, and Irma Pieper Reseburg, third base.

Other girls on the team were: Evelyn Huesterberg Sprenger, Dawn Pippert Kissinger, Shirley Kleinhans Sommer and Ione Steinhardt.

Starting in August we played games about once a week, won games against Howards Grove girls 17-9, Bitter-Neumann 11-10, Sheboygan Falls girls 30-3 then lost to them one week later at Sheboygan Falls, won the 2nd place Sheboygan Leverenz Shoe girls 11-8, and lost games to Millersville Box Company men 21-5, and Sheboygan Dick's Club girls 8-2. For one of our games we didn't have enough girls, so Roland Schomberg played on our girls' team, slid into home plate from third base and broke his ankle.

After this he continued bowling on the Bitter-Neumann team with his sore foot, his average went down, thus receiving more handicap, which led to him receiving the high prize of $50 at the end of the bowling season. This girls' team only played together in 1945 as some of the girls were married the following year and the years, thereafter.

Sheboygan Press
1945
Millersville In 11-8 Girls' Win

A newly organized Millersville Girls' softball club battered Sheboygan's second place team from the Leverenz Shoe Company by an 11 to 8 score in an exhibition game at Millersville last night.

Millersville Baseball Team Year 1945

Sitting front row, left to right: Robert Sprenger, Edward Mueller.

Kneeling, second row, l to r: Robert Mueller, Art Peichl, Ray Bitter, John Kohl, Donald Bitter.

Third row, l to r: Carl Harms, coach, Harold Bitter, Lester Sprenger, James Doro, Arno Sprenger, Adolph Kaemmer, coach.

Fourth row: Arwin (Sonny) Herzog, Carl Sprenger, Ernest Illig, Henry Boeldt, Alfred (Butch) Bitter Jr.

Odds and Ends
1934

First to Apply for a License in New Courthouse

Harvey Schorer of the Town of Herman and Hertha Fiedler of Cleveland, Manitowoc County, were the first couple to apply for marriage license at the new courthouse. He is 25 and she is 23 years old, and they applied for a license Monday afternoon.

Hail Stones Fall at Millersville
Sheboygan Press

While residents of Sheboygan experienced only a few light drops of rain early Friday evening, residents of Millersville and vicinity scurried for shelter as huge hail stones pelted down from the sky.

In some areas, such as along-side barns and buildings, the hail stones were heaped almost a foot high and 12 hours later at 8 o'clock this morning at the farm home of Arthur Heuer, Route 2, Sheboygan, the pellets were still six inches thick in places and could be scooped up in a pail.

The hail storm occurred about 6pm Friday in the county and the pellets were about the size of golf balls.

Moving a House in the 1940s

This was the house of Roy and Mildred Fenn who lived at 1305 Millersville Avenue. It was the house of John Klein, father of Mildred. Mildred recalls in 1940 the house was very close to the road and the road was going to be widened and blacktopped so it had to be moved. Neighbors helped move the house. The house is now over 150 years old. At the time the house had no running water. In 1957 running water and bathroom were added. The house was sold to Brody Stapel in 2006.

John Klein's house before it was moved at left.

Digging out basement to move house.

Norman Klein and Roy Fenn. Albert Oetling's horses at right.

Upper left and upper right: Putting blocks and rollers under the house

Below left: Gust. Wiedemeyer, Albert Oetling, Alfred Doro

Below right: August Knoener and Alfred Doro

Upper left: John Klein

Upper right: Ready to pull the house over

Below left: Pulling the house over

Below right: House on new foundation

The Sheboygan Press
Wednesday, November 20, 1963

Set Cost at $426,930

Sanitary District Residents Voice Approval On Sewer Construction

Millersville-An informal advisory vote by residents of the Howards Grove-Millersville Sanitary District Tuesday evening resulted in a 38 to 4 landslide of approval on the matter of hiring an engineering firm to prepare detailed plans for the proposed sewage system for the community.

The vote was asked by the sanitary district and commissioners, Alfred Bitter, Harvey Sprenger and Gaylord Prange, who conducted the meeting.

The commissioners were assisted by Bob Jones of Donohue and Associate, Inc. and Oscar Eggers of the State Board of Health in presenting a detailed report on the progress of plans for the establishment of sewage treatment facilities in the twin communities of Millersville and Howards Grove.

The meeting held at the Millersville Fire House was attended by about 45 residents of the area and bore little similarity to earlier meetings where strong opposition was voiced from many quarters of the population.

Mr. Sprenger, who opened the meeting, commented that the purpose of the gathering was to present the information gathered thus far and to give residents an opportunity to comment on the project.

Reviews Problem

Mr. Jones of the consulting firm reviewed the history of the Pigeon River pollution problem and commented on the specific requirements of the Howards Grove-Millersville area regarding the construction of a sewage treatment system.

He commented that one of the by-products of such a system would be the knitting together of the two communities into one homogeneous area which could grow together into a much larger municipality then is now possible.

The stabilization pond type of sewage treatment was explained by Mr. Jones and he pointed out that this concept in treatment would not best fit the needs of the area in question while it would probably cost just about as much as a treatment plant.

The commissioners discussed various sewage treatment plants they had visited recently in other Wisconsin communities after which Mr. Jones went into a detailed projected financial analysis of the sewage treatment system.

Estimates Cost

A total cost of $426, 930 which Mr. Jones described as being higher than actual cost, would include 35, 200 feet of sewer servicing 187 homes, three schools, and 19 commercial establishments.

This figure includes $84,800 for the plant and lift station, of which 30 percent would be paid by a federal grant; $69,960 for the north interceptor to Howards Grove, $44,370 for the south interceptor to Howards Grove to Millersville;$80,000 for collection sewers in Millersville and $146,900 for collection sewers in Howards Grove.

Funds for financing the project, as outlined by the Donohue firm, would come from a 29,000 front foot assessment at $2.50 per square foot which would yield $72,500; 209 connection charges at $300 netting $62,700; $2,440 from the federal grant; and a $226, 290 bond issue.

Annual cost of operation would be $26,300, according to the Donohue estimate, which would include $19,500 toward the retirement of the 20-year, four percent bond; $3,000 for operator's salary; $700 for electricity, $200 for supplies; $400 for hauling sludge solids; $400 for sewer maintenance; and $1,500 for depreciation.

Annual revenue for operation would come from a $65 yearly service charge on 206 units amounting to $13,390 and a $65 charge for every 10 pupils in the three schools, totaling $2,925 plus a 4 ½ mill tax on $2,500,00 assessment yielding $11,250.

This would bring in $27,565 a year- slightly more than the anticipated annual cost of the system.

Discuss Water Service

Some discussion was held regarding the cost of installing water mains as well as sewers. Mr. Jones said this would cost just about as much sewer installation but that although there might be some saving in having both jobs done at the same time, state law provides that water mains and sewers cannot be in the same trench.

It was also pointed out that the $300 connection fee and the $2.50 per front foot charge against residents would be permitted to be paid over a five-year period.

The commissioners stated after the meeting that they plan to meet in the next few weeks at which time they will select a consulting firm to prepare a detailed survey and plan for the sewer installation.

The commissioners said it is still uncertain as to the type of bond issue to be made. They said a general obligation bond would require a referendum ballot, probably in the spring elections.

They pointed out that construction would probably begin in November of 1964 and should be completed within a year from then.

Storm Sewer installation 1987 on Millersville Avenue

Being Busy Is No Excuse For Not Being Neighborly

Sheboygan Press, 1999
Dawn Jax Belleau

It's time to set to rest the notion that Sheboygan is a keep-at-arms-length unfriendly town. What I eventually discovered, and what new arrivals and visitors fall to understand, is that Sheboygan is not unfriendly, it's just busy.

It's busy in the way that Millersville was busy when we arrived there in the early 1960s. For those of you who are new to Sheboygan County, Millersville is now part of the larger community, Howards Grove. Like some Brigadoon, Millersville disappeared from the map one day a few years ago; Vanished into the mists of history.

Millersville was not our first choice for establishing a new life. Plymouth, we thought, would be perfect. We preferred Collins or Reed Street, those lovely, tree-shaded streets with sweeping front lawns and wide porches, right out of a Norman Rockwell Illustration. But there were no rental units on Collins Street.

Our flat in Millersville was owned by a pleasant couple, about our age, with a young family. We would become friends, I thought. I also expected the older women in the neighborhood would invite me to an occasional kaffee klatch. I was charmed to hear them speak German as they gathered at the meat counter in the old Bitter-Neumann store on the main street. Once I sent the gathered Fraus into mirthful snorts by asking Alfred Bitter Jr. for four brats pronouncing brat as in naughty child.

The weeks wore on, but there were no invitations for coffee, nor to the parties in our landlords' flat on the first floor. They played a card game I had never heard of called sheepshead or sheeps head. I wasn't sure. When I complained that we were never invited downstairs, Don would remind me that I hated card games. Still, every hoot of laughter, every shout of triumph from those downstairs card parties filled me with a longing to be part of it all.

"They don't even know me," I told Don, "I'm sure they would like me if they just got to know me." "I wouldn't bet on it," he said.

Failing to cheer me with his wit, Don reminded me that the people downstairs were natives with a whole lifetime of accumulated friends and relatives. They simply didn't need more people.

Still, I kept trying. From my Travelers' Guide to Germany, I learned to ask the Fraus at the meat counter 'Wann kommt der Zug?" They told me no trains came through Millersville.

Even as I gained greater command of the German language, commenting on the Fraus' beautiful Blumen in der Garten and praising their green thumbs, I failed to endear myself to those women.

When they occasionally did speak English, I found I had little to add to the conversation. Ja, I was up at 5 and got the wash on the line before 6. Ja, I was up at five, too and the bread is in the oven. What could I say? I had the kids trained to sleep until nine.

During those months in Millersville, I became pregnant. I was delighted even though Sara and Chris were still in diapers. Another little person to talk to, I thought. Loneliness will do that.

Having just returned from Dr. Willard Huibregtse's Sheboygan Clinic office, where he gave me the good news while was chewing on carrot sticks, I was bursting to tell someone. I called my mother in Richland Center. I called Don's mother in Kewaunee, and then set off for Bitter-Neumann's grocery store to buy a celebratory Sara Lee cake. I always tried to sneak one because the Fraus I wanted as friends made their kuchen from scratch.

I stopped at the meat counter to wish the waiting Fraus *Guten Appetit* as they purchased their daily fleisch. Having exhausted my store of German, I turned to leave, but at the sight of Alfred Bitter's welcoming smile, I simply could not contain the joyful news. "I just wanted you to know, Alfred, I'm pregnant!"

Astonished, Alfred dropped his meat cleaver as the gasping Fraus recoiled. That's what loneliness will do.

We moved to End Court in Sheboygan just after Mary was born. Christopher was a year old and Sara was well past two. The neighborhood was full of young families, many of them having come here from some other place. And since their children had no uncles or aunts, grandmas or grandpas in Sheboygan, we formed our own extended our families. We drank coffee at 10 o'clock and hurried home in time to open a can of soup for the school-age kids coming home for lunch.

We filled our lives with family, friends, picnics, politics, and book groups and in time, we were as busy as the Millersville Fraus and the sheepshead players.

Today, I look about our neighborhood and count several new families who have arrived without so much as a welcoming jar of jam from our house to theirs. One of these days, I tell myself, I've just got to make some room in my life for these newcomers.

Otherwise they're going to think Sheboygan is as unfriendly as Millersville (seemed).

Sheboygan Press
Monday, April 22, 1974

A Fatal Turn
Family Outing Ends in Tragedy

By Dawn Belleau
Press Staff Writer

Crushed beneath the heavy branches of an uprooted tree, the Gary Palbrach family car stands at the roadside on Highway 32 at Howards Grove. The Stevens Point family was returning home from a Milwaukee trip when the tornado lifted their car and hurled it in the path of the falling tree. Two hours later, 4-month-old Brian Palbrach died at St. Nicholas Hospital of head injuries.

(Photo by George Marthenze)

There are so many routes from Milwaukee to Stevens Point but fate directed Gary Palbrach and his family through Howards Grove at 5:25pm Sunday when a vicious tornado was gouging the earth and hurling trees.

The Palbrachs, their 4-month-old son Brian, and a niece, Laurie Omitt, 5, were returning from a weekend visit with Milwaukee relatives, including Palbrach's sister, Mrs. James Omitt and her family.

Apparently Palbrach had taken a wrong turn en route to Stevens Point and was moving southward on Highway 32, just north of County JJ, when his car was lifted and projected into the path of a falling tree.

Palbrach told sheriff deputies that the car was actually airborne when the tree fell across it.

Tree Crushes Roof
Heavy limbs crashed through, the roof of the vehicle, inflicting injuries on all four occupants. Two hours later Brian Palbrach died of head injuries at St. Nicholas Hospital.

Sister Augusta Sperl said the child died just after it was determined to transport him to Theda Clark Hospital in Neenah.

Still hospitalized at St. Nicholas today is Laurie Omitt, listed in fair condition with rib and abdominal injuries.

Laurie had expected to spend the next week visiting with her aunt and uncle at their rural Stevens Point home. Laurie's parents arrived at the hospital last night to stay with her, Sister Augusta reported.

Gary Palbrach, 24, and his wife, Christine, 21, were released today. He had been treated for shock, cuts and bruises; she for head lacerations.

Moving along Highway 32 immediately behind the Palbrach car were Harvey and Rachel Parsche, returning to their home at 612 fond du Lac Avenue after visiting their son Phillip in Howards Grove.

Interviewed at his job in the Sheboygan Press composing room today, Parsche said his car had just come over a rise in the road immediately after the tree had fallen on the Palbrach auto.

"Mr. Palbrach was just getting out of the car. He seemed dazed and shocked," said Parsche.

Freed from Wreckage
At about the same time an unidentified motorist pulled up, offering his assistance. He and Parsche worked for the next five minutes to free the remaining three occupants in the car. In order to free Mrs. Palbrach from the front seat, the two men had to pry away bent metal parts and sections of the windshield to get her through the roof portion. The two children were in the rear seat.

The Palbrachs and the Omitt child were taken to the nearby Paul Gillis house, where Mrs. Gillis wrapped and comforted the injured baby.

Rachel Parsche took charge of the five-year-old wrapping her in blankets for shock. Sertich ambulance was called to the Gillis house and the injured were transported to St. Nicholas Hospital.

Mrs. Gillis told The Press today that her family did not see the tree crashing into the car. "We were in the basement because we knew the tornado was coming," she said.

"We came up immediately and I held the baby all the while until the ambulance arrived. It was frightening for all of us. About the baby . . . We were hoping for the best."

Gary and Christine Palbrach had been married for two years and Brian was their only child. They live in the Town of Stockton near Stevens Point where Palbrach is employed at the Bake-Rite Company.

By Arline Hoppe

On a Saturday afternoon in April 2005, a young couple saw us outside and stopped to ask if we could tell them the spot of the accident where the tornado in 1974 took down the tree. We told them although we lived right next door, we weren't home when the tornado came through here, as we had left the day before on a tour to Hawaii with about 20 other people from the surrounding area.

The young lady was Laurie Omitt (now Kluck), the five-year- old who was also in the car and said she couldn't remember much.

The day after the tornado we heard by television in Hawaii that a tornado had gone through Sheboygan County. Then one week later we saw a copy of the Sheboygan Press which was sent to two young girls from Sheboygan by their parents. It was a shock to see our house in the background of the accident.

We and all of our neighbors had quite a bit of damage, but we were so thankful we still had our homes. Several people to the northeast of us had lost their homes. Laurie than asked about Barb Gillis, but not finding her home, left a note and both Barb and I have corresponded with her.

Laurie informed me she would be very interested in buying the "Millersville" book.

Made in the USA
Middletown, DE
14 November 2021